Secured & Locked Down

Mastering The Modern Wealth Game with IUL

Brandon E. Beal

Published by Brexus Publishing Co.

2024

Secured & Locked Down: Mastering the Modern Wealth Game with IUL

Published by Brexus Publishing Co.
312 W. 2nd St
Casper, WY 82601

ISBN (Paperback): 978-8-9909695-2-0

Library of Congress Control Number: 2024112345

This is a work of nonfiction. The names, characters, businesses, places, events, and incidents are either the products of the author's imagination or used in a fictitious manner. Any resemblance to actual persons, living or dead, or actual events is purely coincidental.

Editing by: Brandon E. Beal

Printed in the United States of America

First Edition: September 2024

For more information about the author, please visit www.securedandlocked.com

Preface

Welcome to the journey of understanding and harnessing the power of Index Universal Life Insurance through our comprehensive guide, "Benefits of Using Index Universal Life Insurance: A Tapestry of Tax-Efficient Wealth Accumulation and Protection." My journey as a licensed financial professional and insurance advisor has been marked by witnessing the profound transformation that strategic financial planning can bring to individuals and families. It is this transformative power that has motivated me to demystify the complexities surrounding Index Universal Life Insurance (IUL) and bring to light its potential through clear explanations, vivid real-life examples, and actionable insights designed to cater to your unique financial canvas.

"Investing is not nearly as difficult as it looks. Successful investing involves doing a few things right and avoiding serious mistakes." This insight from John C. Bogle, the founder of Vanguard Group, encapsulates the essence of what we aim to achieve in this book. By navigating the intricacies of IUL, we hope to guide you towards making informed decisions that resonate with your financial aspirations.

Furthermore, Benjamin Franklin's timeless wisdom, "An investment in knowledge pays the best interest," stands at the core of our mission. We believe that empowering you with knowledge about IUL will serve as a cornerstone in building and protecting your wealth efficiently.

Acknowledgments

First and foremost, I want to thank my amazing wife, Ashley. Honey, thank you for putting up with my late-night writing sessions, endless cans of Monster and Rockstar energy drinks, and occasional bouts of writer's block-induced grumpiness. Your unwavering support and love have been my driving force, even when you had to remind me to take a shower. This book wouldn't have been possible without your endless encouragement and your ability to laugh at my worst jokes.

To my wonderful daughter, Brielle, you are my inspiration and my motivation. Your boundless energy and curiosity keep me on my toes, and your laughter with your one dimple is the best remedy after a long day. Every time you see me typing, you're probably wondering what the heck I'm doing. I hope you know it's all for you. One day, you'll be able to read this and realize that yes, Daddy was writing something important (at least he thinks so).

Thank you both for being my rock, my source of endless joy, and for occasionally distracting me just enough to keep me sane. This book is dedicated to you, with all my love and a little bit of humor.

Disclaimer

The contents of this book are presented to you as an educational odyssey, designed to illuminate the path but not to prescribe a specific course of action. The information herein should not be interpreted as financial, investment, or tax advice. All financial excursions entail nuances and complexities unique to each individual's life story. Therefore, before embarking on any financial decision, it is of paramount importance to engage with a qualified financial advisor or tax professional. Such consultation ensures that your decisions are tailored to align with the unique contours of your personal circumstances, thereby crafting a strategy that not only meets but exceeds your needs.

By diving into this book, you are taking the first step towards demystifying the realms of financial planning and protection. Let this be a guide not just to the accumulation of wealth, but to understanding the art of preserving it through thoughtful and informed strategies. Welcome to a journey towards financial enlightenment and empowerment.

Table of Contents

Chapter 1: **We've Been Duped**

Chapter 2: **The Looming Retirement Savings Crisis**

Chapter 3: **Enter the World of Indexed Universal Life (IUL)**

Chapter 4: **IUL: Your Locked & Loaded Retirement Weapon**

Chapter 5: **Challenging the Status Quo: "Buy Term and Invest the Difference"**

Chapter 6: **Toss Your Kiddo's 529**

Chapter 7: **Infinite Banking: Mastering Financial Freedom**

Chapter 8: **What the IUL Haters Say**

Chapter 9: **You Only Fail When You Fail to Plan**

Chapter 10: **Legends and Legacies: Titans of Life Insurance**

Chapter 11: **Inspiring Real-Life Success Stories**

Chapter 12: **High Income Earners**

Chapter 13: **The Rich & Famous: CEOs, Actors & Athletes**

Chapter 14: **BOLI: Here's Where the Banks Stash Their Cash**

Chapter 15: **Master Your Finances with IUL**

Rave Reviews

"Just like on the football field, where having the right playbook and strategy makes all the difference, this book is the ultimate playbook for financial success. It breaks down complex financial concepts into easy-to-understand strategies, much like a coach simplifying a game plan for his team. This is a must-read for anyone looking to tackle their financial goals and score big in life. It's packed with insights that will help you navigate the financial field and come out a champion."

- Shawn Merriman, Former NFL Pro Bowl Star and San Diego Charger

"Ernst and Young recently published a whitepaper saying the optimal retirement portfolio should consist of 30% Cash Value Life Insurance, 30% Income Annuities and 40% Investments. In his book 'Secured & Locked Down', Brandon Beal clearly explains why Life Insurance and all of its significant tax advantages should play a key role in your retirement."

-Tom Hegna, Retired Lieutenant Colonel, Author Speaker and THE Retirement Income Expert

"Brandon's deep understanding of wealth accumulation planning and his innovation to the preservation of wealth are truly unparralled. 'Secured & Locked Down' is a masterclass in leveraging IUL to secure your financial future. This book is a testament to Brandon's expertise and his ability to simplify complex concepts, making it an essential read for anyone serious about mastering their finances."

-Bradley Beal, 3X NBA All-Star and All NBA Team

Introduction

I'm Brandon, and I'm thrilled to embark on this journey with you. I've spent years in the financial industry, helping folks just like you navigate the often murky waters of retirement planning. And let me tell you, there's one tool that stands out from the rest: Indexed Universal Life Insurance (IUL).

So why did I write this book? Well, I've seen too many people struggle with their finances, especially when it comes to planning for retirement. The traditional methods don't always cut it anymore. IUL is different—it's powerful, flexible, and can truly change your financial future. My goal is to make this complex topic simple and show you how IUL can work for you.

By the end of this book, you'll understand how IUL works, why it's different from other retirement plans, and how it can offer you the financial security and peace of mind you deserve. Ready to get started? Let's dive in!

Chapter 1: You've Been Duped

Meet John. John did everything by the book — graduated from college, landed a decent job, and diligently contributed to his 401(k). He was confident he'd retire comfortably. But as he approached retirement, John realized his savings wouldn't be enough. Market fluctuations had eroded his nest egg, and unexpected expenses kept cropping up. Sound familiar?

We've all been told the same story: work hard, save in your 401(k), and you'll retire comfortably. But for many, this vision is a mirage. The reality is that traditional retirement plans have inherent flaws. They're often exposed to market volatility, limited by contribution caps, and burdened with tax implications.

The Reality of 401(k) Plans

Let's dive deeper into the pitfalls of 401(k) plans. According to data from the Investment Company Institute, only 52% of American households have retirement accounts, and the median balance is shockingly low. For those between the ages of 55 and

64, the median 401(k) balance is around $120,000. This might sound like a decent amount, but when you consider that financial advisors recommend having at least eight times your annual salary saved by retirement, it's clear that most people are falling short.

Market Volatility: The Silent Killer of Retirement Savings

Market volatility is one of the biggest threats to your retirement savings. Let's look at some significant events in recent history that have severely impacted retirement accounts:

The Dot-Com Bubble (2000-2002)

The early 2000s saw the burst of the dot-com bubble, which led to the NASDAQ losing nearly 78% of its value. During this period, many Americans saw their 401(k) and IRA balances drop significantly. On average, retirement accounts lost about 20-30% of their value during the dot-com crash.

September 11, 2001

The terrorist attacks on September 11, 2001, caused immediate turmoil in the financial markets. The stock market was closed for several days, and when it reopened, the S&P 500 fell nearly 12% over the next five trading days. Many Americans saw their 401(k) and IRA balances decline by around 10-15% in the immediate aftermath.

The 2008 Financial Crisis

The 2008 financial crisis is a prime example of market volatility's devastating impact. The S&P 500 lost nearly 57% of its value from its peak in October 2007 to its trough in March

2009. During this period, the average 401(k) account balance for people in their 50s dropped by 25-30%. To put it into perspective, if you had $500,000 saved in your 401(k), your savings could have plummeted to around $350,000 or even less.

COVID-19 Pandemic (2020)

The COVID-19 pandemic caused unprecedented market volatility in early 2020. The S&P 500 dropped by about 34% from its peak in February to its low in March. During this period, the average American 401(k) and IRA balances fell by approximately 20%. While the market eventually recovered, the initial shock and uncertainty caused significant stress for those nearing retirement.

Recovering from Market Losses

Recovering from significant market losses is not a straightforward process. The percentage gain required to recover from a loss is often much higher than the percentage of the initial loss. For example:

- 10% Loss: Requires an 11% gain to recover.

- 20% Loss: Requires a 25% gain to recover.

- 30% Loss: Requires a 43% gain to recover.

- 40% Loss: Requires a 67% gain to recover.

- 50% Loss: Requires a 100% gain to recover.

Considering the time it takes for the market to recover, let's look at historical data:

- After the dot-com bubble, it took the NASDAQ over 15 years to reach its previous high.

- Following the 2008 financial crisis, the S&P 500 took about 4.5 years to recover its losses.

These timelines highlight the importance of having a diversified and resilient financial plan that can withstand market downturns without derailing your retirement goals.

The Limitations of Contribution Caps

401(k) plans also have contribution limits. As of 2024, the maximum annual contribution limit for 401(k) plans is $23,000 for those under 50 and $30,000 for those 50 and older. While these limits might seem high, they can be restrictive for high earners or those who start saving later in life and need to catch up.

Let's say you start contributing to your 401(k) at age 35 with the goal of retiring at 65. If you contribute the maximum amount each year, assuming an average annual return of 7%, you could accumulate around $2 million by retirement. However, this doesn't account for potential market downturns, taxes, or inflation, all of which can erode your savings.

The Tax Burden: An Unwelcome Surprise

Taxes are another significant drawback of traditional retirement accounts like 401(k)s. While contributions to a 401(k) are tax-deferred, you'll pay taxes on withdrawals during retirement. This means you're potentially paying higher taxes in retirement, especially if tax rates increase or if your income needs remain high.

Consider a retiree with a $1 million 401(k) balance who needs $80,000 per year to maintain their lifestyle. If they're in a 22% tax bracket, they'll owe $17,600 in taxes, leaving them with $62,400. Over a 20-year retirement, this adds up to $352,000 in taxes, significantly reducing their nest egg.

The Illusion of Security: Pension Plans and Social Security

Pension plans and Social Security are often touted as reliable sources of retirement income. However, the reality is that these sources are not as secure as they once were.

Pensions are becoming increasingly rare in the private sector. According to the Bureau of Labor Statistics, only 14% of private-sector workers had access to a defined benefit pension plan in 2023, compared to 60% in the early 1980s. Even for those who do have pensions, there's no guarantee that the company will be able to fulfill its promises. Many companies have underfunded pension plans, and if they go bankrupt, retirees could lose their benefits.

Social Security, on the other hand, is facing its own challenges. The Social Security Trustees Report projects that the trust fund reserves will be depleted by 2033. Without changes to the program, benefits could be reduced by 23% at that time. For many retirees, Social Security is a critical source of income, and any reduction in benefits could be devastating.

The Overlooked Costs of Healthcare in Retirement

Another often-overlooked aspect of retirement planning is healthcare costs. According to a 2023 report by Fidelity, the average 65-year-old couple retiring today will need approximately $315,000 to cover healthcare expenses throughout retirement. This includes premiums for Medicare Part B and D, as well as out-of-pocket expenses. This figure does not include potential long-term care costs, which can be substantial.

Long-term care, such as nursing home or in-home care, is not covered by Medicare. According to the U.S. Department of Health and Human Services, about 70% of people over 65 will need some form of long-term care services during their lives. The average cost of a private room in a nursing home was over $100,000 per year in 2023. These costs can quickly deplete retirement savings if not planned for adequately.

Inflation: The Invisible Threat

Inflation is another factor that can erode the purchasing power of your retirement savings. Even a modest inflation rate of 2-3% can significantly impact your savings over a 20- or 30-year retirement. For example, if you retire with $1 million and inflation averages 3% per year, the purchasing power of your savings will be reduced by half in about 24 years. This means that what costs $50,000 today will cost about $100,000 in 24 years.

The Emotional Toll of Financial Insecurity

Financial insecurity in retirement can also take a significant emotional toll. The stress of not knowing if you have enough saved, the fear of outliving your savings, and the anxiety over potential market downturns can negatively impact your mental and physical health. According to a 2022 survey by the Employee Benefit Research Institute, nearly half of retirees report feeling less confident about their financial future compared to previous years.

The False Sense of Security from Employer Matches

Many employees rely on employer matches to boost their 401(k) savings. While employer matches are a great benefit, they are not a guaranteed source of retirement income. Companies can change their match policies at any time, and employees who leave their job before being fully vested may lose part or all of their employer contributions. It's important to have a retirement plan that doesn't solely rely on employer matches to ensure financial security.

Actionable Steps for a Secure Retirement:

1. Diversify Your Portfolio:

   - Don't rely solely on 401(k) plans. Explore other investment options such as Indexed Universal Life (IUL) insurance policies, annuities, and real estate to spread risk.

2. Plan for Healthcare Costs:

   - Consider purchasing long-term care insurance and saving specifically for healthcare expenses to cover potential high costs in retirement.

3. Stay Informed on Social Security:

   - Keep up-to-date with changes in Social Security policies and plan for potential reductions in benefits.

4. Inflation-Proof Your Savings:

   - Invest in assets that can potentially outpace inflation, such as stocks, real estate, or inflation-protected securities.

5. Regularly Review Your Financial Plan:

   - Schedule annual reviews of your financial plan with a trusted advisor to adjust for changes in the market and your personal circumstances.

A New Path Forward

John's story is all too common. Many people diligently save for retirement, only to find that their traditional retirement plans fall short of their expectations. Understanding the limitations of these plans and the risks involved can help you make more informed decisions about your financial future.

In the next chapter, we'll delve deeper into the looming retirement savings crisis and explore why so many people are unprepared for retirement. We'll look at the statistics, analyze the trends, and discuss the steps you can take to protect yourself and your loved ones.

By focusing on the inherent flaws and limitations of traditional retirement savings accounts, this chapter aims to highlight the importance of exploring alternative strategies for a secure retirement.

Chapter 2: The Looming Retirement Savings Crisis

Labor economists and retirement experts have long sounded the alarm about the looming retirement savings crisis, emphasizing its potential to destabilize the financial security of future retirees. Recent reports from reputable organizations like the National Institute on Retirement Security (NIRS) provide empirical evidence of the severity of the situation. These reports reveal alarming statistics: almost half of working-age households in the United States have no retirement savings whatsoever. Such findings corroborate the warnings of renowned experts who have cautioned about the precariousness of Americans' retirement preparedness.

Furthermore, the data paints a stark picture of the inadequacy of retirement savings among those nearing retirement age. For instance, according to the Economic Policy Institute, the median retirement savings for families headed by individuals aged 56-61 is only $21,000. This is a critical issue considering the traditional 4% withdrawal rule, which suggests that retirees can withdraw 4% of their retirement savings annually to sustain themselves. For many, this rule proves woefully inadequate due to increasing life expectancy, inflation, and skyrocketing healthcare costs.

Social Security and Its Shortcomings

Let's face it: relying solely on Social Security to fund your retirement is like expecting a tricycle to win the Tour de France. The average monthly Social Security benefit for retired workers was around $1,500 in 2023. This amount barely covers basic living expenses, let alone healthcare and unforeseen costs. As the ratio of workers to retirees decreases, the sustainability of Social Security is increasingly questioned, making it unreliable as a sole source of retirement income.

The 401(k) Plan: Challenges and Limitations

Consider John, who has diligently contributed to his 401(k) plan throughout his career, aiming to build a nest egg for retirement. By the time John reaches retirement age at 65, his 401(k) account has grown to $500,000 through a combination of his contributions and investment returns. But here's the kicker: 401(k) plans have annual contribution limits, currently set at $22,500 for individuals under 50 as of 2024, which may restrict the amount he can save for retirement each year. Additionally, individuals aged 50 and older are allowed to make catch-up contributions, which are currently capped at an additional $7,500 as of 2024. These limits, along with market volatility and potential employer-specific restrictions, can seriously hinder adequate retirement savings. It's like running a marathon with one leg tied to a tree – you're not going to get very far.

But this is what happens when our government takes control of what we do with our money out of our hands. This is what happens when we let an outdated system dictate how much money we can earn, save, invest, and withdraw. How's that fair?

IRAs and Roth IRAs: Contribution Limits and Inflation Impact

Roth IRAs offer tax advantages but come with specific income limitations and contribution caps. For instance:

- **Single Filers:**
    - Maximum contribution of $6,500 is allowed for incomes up to $138,000.
    - Contribution phases out for incomes between $138,000 and $153,000.
    - No contributions are allowed for incomes above $153,000.

- **Married Filing Jointly:**
    - Maximum contribution of $6,500 is allowed for incomes up to $218,000.
    - Contribution phases out for incomes between $218,000 and $228,000.
    - No contributions are allowed for incomes above $228,000.

The impact of inflation further erodes the purchasing power of retirement savings over time. For instance, if Maria plans to retire at 65 and expects to live for another 20 years, she'll need to ensure that her retirement savings can sustain her standard of living over that period. Due to inflation, the purchasing power of her $500,000 retirement savings would significantly diminish over time, potentially affecting her ability to maintain her desired standard of living. Inflation is the silent thief in the night, sneaking away with your hard-earned dollars while you sleep.

The Inadequacy of the 4% Rule

The traditional 4% rule, which suggests that retirees can withdraw 4% of their retirement savings annually, is increasingly seen as inadequate. This rule doesn't account for increasing life expectancy, healthcare costs, and inflation, which can erode retirement savings faster than anticipated. As a result, many retirees may face financial insecurity and may need to work into their late 70s or beyond, as my grandmother did, to make ends meet. Imagine celebrating your 75th birthday by blowing out the candles at your office desk – not exactly the golden years we dream of.

Thrift Savings Plan (TSP)

The Thrift Savings Plan (TSP) is a retirement savings and investment plan designed for federal employees and members of the uniformed services, including the Ready Reserve. Established in 1986, TSP aims to provide retirement income and supplement traditional federal retirement benefits, similar to private sector 401(k) plans. It offers various investment options, including government securities, fixed income, common stock, small-cap stock, international stock, and lifecycle funds.

While the TSP provides valuable benefits such as tax-deferred contributions, Roth options, and matching contributions for Federal Employees Retirement System (FERS) participants, it has significant limitations. One major drawback is its exposure to market risk; TSP funds, especially the C, S, and I Funds, are subject to market fluctuations, which can result in significant losses during downturns. Additionally, TSP offers limited investment options compared to private retirement plans, restricting participants from investing in individual stocks, real estate, or other alternative assets.

Moreover, the TSP imposes strict withdrawal restrictions and penalties for early withdrawals before age 59½, limiting financial flexibility. Required Minimum Distributions (RMDs) starting at age 72 can force participants to withdraw funds even when they prefer to leave their money invested. Lastly, while contributions are tax-deferred, all withdrawals from traditional TSP accounts are taxed as ordinary income, potentially leading to substantial tax liabilities in retirement. It's like trying to enjoy your favorite dessert with a giant tax fork hovering over it.

Conclusion

Given the limitations of traditional retirement vehicles like Social Security, 401(k)s, IRAs, and the TSP, it's crucial to explore alternative strategies. Chapter 3 will delve into innovative approaches like Indexed Universal Life Insurance (IUL) and other non-traditional investment vehicles that have the potential to revolutionize retirement planning. By challenging conventional wisdom and embracing forward-thinking solutions, individuals can navigate the complexities of retirement savings with confidence and ensure a secure and prosperous future.

Chapter 3: Enter the World of Index Universal Life Insurance (IUL)

Name me one financial vehicle that can do what the IUL can do... don't worry I'll wait. You can't. It's an unbeatable force; like MJ in Game 6s or Tom Brady in Super Bowl LI. These two GOATs have a relentless desire to win and outlast, and so does Index Universal Life. But to understand it today, let's go back into the past a little bit.

History of Cash Value Life Insurance

The concept of cash value life insurance has a rich history dating back to the early 19th century. Whole life insurance policies were among the first to be introduced, offering policyholders a guaranteed death benefit and an opportunity to accumulate cash value over time through consistent premium payments and interest earnings. The percentage of cash value earnings in these policies typically ranged from 2% to 4% annually. These policies were revolutionary in their promise of financial security and predictability, providing a dual benefit that catered to both protection and savings. Two to four percent, good but not great.

Throughout the 20th century, the life insurance industry evolved, introducing various forms of cash value life insurance. Universal life insurance was developed, providing greater flexibility in premium payments and death benefits. Variable universal life insurance took this a step further by allowing policyholders to invest in a range of sub-accounts, akin to mutual funds, thereby offering potential for higher returns along with increased risk. The VUL was introduced in the 1980s and by the '90s it took off, when the US stock market and economy were booming into the year 2000. During this time, you could invest your money in almost anything, and it was likely to grow. However, the subsequent bust in the early 2000s resulted in substantial losses, highlighting the inherent risks and volatility of VUL policies and 401(k)s alike, tied to market performance. This period marked a significant shift towards offering consumers more control and options tailored to their individual financial goals and risk tolerance.

Introduction of Index Universal Life Insurance (IUL)

Index Universal Life Insurance (IUL) emerged as a further evolution of cash value life insurance, blending the stability and guarantees of traditional whole life insurance with the potential for higher returns linked to stock market performance. Introduced in 1997 by Transamerica, IUL was crafted in response to consumer demand for more robust retirement savings vehicles that could offer both growth and protection. As market volatility became a growing concern, particularly after events like the dot-com bubble and the 2008 financial crisis, there was a clear need for products that could safeguard principal while still providing opportunities for growth.

IUL was designed to address these needs by linking the cash value growth to the performance of selected stock market indexes (e.g., S&P 500, NASDAQ, DOW JONES). This innovation allowed policyholders to benefit from the upward potential of the market while mitigating downside risk, thanks to the built-in floors that prevent negative returns. This unique structure made IUL an attractive option for a wide range of investors, from those nearing retirement to younger individuals seeking long-term growth with a safety net and no limitations.

How Indexed Universal Life Insurance Works

Indexed Universal Life Insurance is a type of permanent life insurance that combines a death benefit with a cash value component that earns interest based on the performance of a stock market index. As a universal life policy, just like its predecessors, it provides flexibility in premium payments and death benefits, allowing policyholders to adjust these elements according to their financial circumstances and goals.

The cash value in an IUL policy is tied to one or more stock indexes, such as the S&P 500, Barclays, or Dow Jones Industrial Average. These indices track a group of stocks and reflect the overall performance of the market. Insurance companies credit interest to policyholders based on the performance of these indexes. When the index performs well, the cash value in the policy grows, potentially offering higher returns than traditional fixed interest products.

Downside Protection

When you think of the perfect savings vehicle, when you think of the perfect investment component, one thing that should come to your mind is, "I wish there was something out there I could put my money into and not have to worry about losing a single penny if the stock market goes belly up." Guess what? That component exists!

Warren Buffet's advice, "Rule No. 1: Never lose money. Rule No. 2: Never forget rule No.1," perfectly aligns with the protective and growth-oriented nature of IUL. By safeguarding your capital while still providing opportunities for growth, IUL offers a balanced approach to financial security.

A critical feature of IUL policies is downside protection, which ensures that the cash value does not decrease due to negative market performance. This is achieved through the implementation of "floors". The floor is the minimum interest rate guaranteed by the policy, often set at 0%, meaning that even in the worst market conditions, the policyholder's cash value will not decrease. For example, during the severe market downturns in 2008 and the 2020 COVID-19 pandemic, when traditional retirement accounts experienced significant losses, IUL policies would have credited a 0% return, thus protecting the policyholder's capital. This feature is especially appealing to risk-averse individuals who seek the security of knowing that their investment will not lose value. So essentially, Zero is your Hero. Your Roth, your friend's 401(k), and your cousin's TSP all took a hit of 34% during COVID. My own personal IUL had a 19% return and my wife Ashley's policy had a 21% return. Let that sink in for a little bit.

Growth Potential

You probably wish there was a vehicle you could invest in that gave you uncapped growth. That too, along with downside protection, exists with IUL.

In addition to downside protection, IUL policies offer the potential for significant growth. The cash value grows based on the performance of the selected stock index, with the interest credited to the policy reflecting the index's performance. If the market has an annual return of 10%, the policyholder's account is credited with a 10% gain. In years of exceptional market performance, such as a 30% return, the policyholder's account reflects that full gain, subject to the policy's cap rate. This ability to participate in market gains while being shielded from losses makes IUL a compelling option for those seeking both growth and security.

Flexibility in Premium Payments

You probably wish you had a vehicle that allowed you more control over your contributions; probably wish you had something where you were the captain of your own ship, not your employer or the government. As with great growth and downside protection, you also have flexibility with IUL.

IUL policies are designed with flexibility in mind, allowing policyholders to adjust their premium payments based on their financial situation. This flexibility is particularly beneficial during times of financial uncertainty or fluctuating income. Policyholders can increase or decrease their contributions as needed, ensuring that the policy remains in force while adapting to changing financial circumstances. This adaptability can be a crucial advantage for individuals who experience variable income streams or unexpected financial challenges.

Tax Advantages

Lord knows we wish to sweet baby Jesus we didn't have to pay taxes on trying to grow our money so we can have a nice comfy retirement. What if I told you that with IUL, Uncle Sam can't put his sticky fingers in your pockets trying to grab 30-40%?

IUL policies offer several tax benefits that can enhance retirement savings and wealth accumulation. The cash value in an IUL policy grows on a tax-deferred basis. Additionally, policyholders can access the policy's cash value through loans on a tax-free basis. This tax efficiency makes IUL an attractive tool for retirement planning, as it allows policyholders to maximize their savings and income while minimizing their tax burden. Google "IRS 7702," you'll thank me later.

Compound Interest

One of the most powerful aspects of IUL policies is the effect of compound interest. Compound interest is the process of earning interest on both the principal amount and the accumulated interest from previous periods. This compounding effect can lead to exponential growth over time, significantly enhancing the cash value of the policy. By leveraging compound interest, policyholders can build substantial wealth and secure a strong financial foundation for their future.

The IUL vs. 401(k)

Distinctions Between IUL and 401(k)

1. **Market Exposure:** Traditional 401(k) plans are exposed to market downturns, resulting in potential losses. In contrast, IUL policies offer protection from market losses through their guaranteed floors. Remember, zero is hero.

2.   **Loan Flexibility:** IUL policies provide greater flexibility for borrowing against the policy's cash value compared to 401(k) plans, which have stricter borrowing rules and potential penalties.

3.   **Early Access Penalties:** 401(k) withdrawals before age 59½ incur a 10% penalty and income taxes (minimum 20%), while IUL policies allow for penalty-free loans within your policy.

4.   **Taxable Distributions:** Distributions or income from a 401(k) are subject to income taxes, whereas loans from an IUL policy are tax-free, providing a more tax-efficient income stream.

5.   **Contribution Limits:** 401(k) plans have strict annual contribution limits of $23,000 today, while IUL policies do not have such restrictive limits, allowing for greater flexibility in funding the policy.

6.   **Contractual Guarantees:** IUL policies include contractual guarantees that help preserve earning power and provide financial stability during working years.

7.   **Customization:** IUL policies can be tailored with various riders to address specific needs, such as chronic illness, disability, and other personalized requirements.

Additional Advantages of IUL

1.   **No Contribution Limits:** Unlike traditional retirement accounts, IUL policies do not impose limits on the amount of contributions, allowing policyholders to invest more and grow their wealth without restrictions.

2. **Guaranteed Life Insurance:** IUL policies provide guaranteed life insurance coverage that cannot be revoked, ensuring that the policyholder's beneficiaries receive the death benefit.

3. **Principal Protection:** IUL policies protect the principal from market recessions, ensuring that the policyholder's investment remains secure even during economic downturns.

4. **Tax-Free Withdrawals:** Withdrawals from an IUL during retirement are tax-free, allowing policyholders to maximize their income without increasing their tax liability.

IRS Independence

IUL policies offer a level of privacy and simplicity in managing retirement funds, as they are not subject to the same IRS scrutiny as traditional retirement accounts. There is no requirement to file paperwork or report withdrawals, providing a hassle-free approach to accessing retirement income.

Conclusion

The evolution of cash value life insurance, culminating in the introduction of Index Universal Life Insurance (IUL), has significantly transformed financial planning and retirement savings strategies. From its early beginnings in the 19th century to its current form, cash value life insurance has continuously adapted to meet the changing needs of consumers.

IUL represents a major milestone in this evolution, offering a unique combination of downside protection, growth potential, flexibility, and tax advantages. These features make IUL an indispensable tool for individuals looking to secure their financial futures and achieve long-term goals.

Why Haven't You Heard About IUL?

Well, if IUL is so great, how come I haven't heard about it? Simple: the government doesn't want you to know about it. They want you in 401(k)s and other traditional accounts so they can get their hands on their 40%. Widespread adoption of IULs would change the landscape of tax revenue and investments.

In the next chapter, we will explore the superiority of IUL over traditional retirement savings vehicles and investment strategies in more detail. Understanding the distinct advantages of IUL is crucial for anyone looking to take control of their financial future and ensure a secure and prosperous retirement.

Chapter 4: IUL: Your Locked & Loaded Retirement Weapon

The Beacon of Financial Security

Picture this: you're navigating the jungle of retirement planning, and out of nowhere, a bright beacon appears, guiding you through the treacherous terrain. That beacon? It's Indexed Universal Life Insurance (IUL). It's not just another fancy product; it's your trusty sidekick in the quest for financial stability and peace of mind.

Market Immunity: The Superpower You Didn't Know You Needed

In the world of investments, market volatility is like that unpredictable villain in every superhero movie — never a good thing. Enter IUL, the superhero with the power to shield you from those wild market swings. While others are freaking out during economic rollercoasters, you're chilling with your IUL, knowing your hard-earned money is safe from the market's tantrums.

Remember when Einstein said, "In the middle of difficulty lies opportunity"? Well, IUL took that advice and ran with it. IUL's design means you're protected during market downturns. So when the financial world goes to pieces—like in 2008 or during the 2020 COVID-19 crisis—your IUL policy is your financial fortress. You might not be rolling in dough during a crash, but with a 0% return, you're not losing a cent either. Zero is the new hero, folks!

And it's not all about avoiding losses—it's about snagging gains, too. My policy with Fidelity and Guarantee Life pulled a cool 19% return during the COVID-19 pandemic. My wife's policy did even better with 21%. Take that, market chaos!

Flexibility and Freedom: No Handcuffs Here

Unlike traditional retirement accounts that slap you with penalties for early withdrawals, IUL is like the cool parent—letting you access your funds without a fuss. Got a sudden financial need? No problem. Want to put more into your policy than your 401(k) allows? Go right ahead. IUL is all about giving you control over your savings.

Growth Potential: Channeling Your Inner Warren Buffett

Imagine your wealth growing as the S&P 500 climbs. With IUL, that's your reality. Unlike boring old savings accounts with fixed returns, IUL lets you ride the waves of market growth, potentially turning your retirement fund into a treasure chest.

Tax-Free Income Through Policy Loans: The Sneaky Genius Move

Think of a policy loan from your IUL like a secret stash you can tap into without Uncle Sam noticing. It's like a HELOC for your life insurance. Need cash? Borrow against your policy's cash value without triggering a taxable event. It's like having your cake and eating it too, but without the IRS crashing the party.

Patrick Kelly sums it up perfectly in his book *Tax-Free Retirement*: "It's not what you make, it's what you keep that counts." And IULs are all about helping you keep more of what you earn by giving you tax-free income. Genius, right?

Examples of Policy Loan Uses: Living the Dream

Here are a few ways you can use those tax-free policy loans from your IUL:

- **Family Vacation**: Treat your family to that dream vacation without worrying about the cost.

- **Children's College Expenses**: Send your kids to college without the burden of student loans.

- **Luxury Items**: Fancy a new car or a yacht? Go ahead, splurge without guilt.

- **Real Estate Investments**: Grow your wealth by investing in real estate.

- **Emergency Expenses**: Handle unexpected medical bills or emergencies without dipping into other savings.

- **Business Opportunities**: Fund your next big business idea with ease.

Expert Opinions: The Pros Know Best

David McKnight, author of *The Power of Zero*, calls IUL a "powerful tool for retirement planning" because of its flexibility and tax advantages. Translation: IUL is like the Swiss Army knife of financial planning — versatile and incredibly useful.

Case Studies: Real-Life Superheroes

- **The Smith Family**: John and Sarah Smith used their IUL to build a solid financial base for retirement and cover their kids' college costs. Talk about a win-win!

- **Retirement Reinvented**: Jane, a 60-year-old retiree, used her IUL to cover unexpected medical expenses without penalties. Flexibility for the win!

Conclusion: Your Financial Superhero Awaits

Indexed Universal Life Insurance isn't just another tool in the retirement planning shed — it's the whole toolkit. Offering market-linked growth, protection from downturns, tax benefits, and unparalleled flexibility, IUL is your ticket to a secure financial future. Embrace the power of IUL and stride confidently into retirement with your finances in check and your worries left in the dust.

But don't stop there. In the next chapter, we'll challenge the status quo and debunk some of the most popular financial strategies out there. It's time to rethink conventional wisdom and discover why IUL is the game-changer you've been looking for. Get ready to see how IUL stacks up against traditional plans and why it just might be the best-kept secret in retirement planning. Buckle up, because we're about to shake things up!

Chapter 5: Challenging the Status Quo: "Buy Term and Invest the Difference"

Shaking Up the Financial Jungle

In the wild, unpredictable world of financial planning, there's this ancient, almost sacred mantra: "Buy term and invest the difference." Financial gurus like Dave Ramsey and Suze Orman have preached it for decades like it's the holy grail of fiscal wisdom. Sounds simple, right? Get some cheap term life insurance, invest what you save, and voila! You're a financial wizard. But hold your horses — this old chestnut has more cracks than a dropped smartphone screen.

The Origin Story: Peeling Back the Layers

Flashback to the 1970s: Arthur Williams was the guy who kicked off this movement. He pitched a plan that made life insurance affordable while pushing you to be an investment whiz. But guess what? The world's changed a tad since disco ruled and bell-bottoms were in vogue. Williams' model, while groundbreaking then, doesn't quite match up with today's financial battlefield.

The Concept Unpacked

At its heart, this strategy separates protection from investment. Get yourself some term life insurance (cheap and cheerful) and funnel the saved cash into other investments. It's based on the belief that you'll be a disciplined investor and the market will always be your friend. But Warren Buffett, in all his sage-like wisdom, once said, "Do not save what is left after spending, but spend what is left after saving." This reveals the first major flaw: this strategy demands superhuman discipline, something most of us mere mortals lack.

The Reality Behind 'Invest the Difference'

Here's the kicker: that extra cash you're supposed to invest? It often disappears into the black hole of everyday expenses. Benjamin Franklin's old saying, "Beware of little expenses; a small leak will sink a great ship," couldn't be more spot-on. The truth is, life happens, and most people don't have the financial discipline to invest consistently. Instead, they end up spending that difference on, well, life — unplanned purchases, emergencies, or that irresistible daily latte.

A Closer Examination

Sure, for a disciplined few, this strategy could work wonders. But term insurance is like that one friend who vanishes when things get tough — it's temporary. As you age, it gets pricier, and before you know it, you're stuck paying more or losing coverage altogether. Plus, only about 2% of term policies ever pay out. Yep, you read that right — 2%. It's like buying a lottery ticket with worse odds.

The Untold Implications

Enter Indexed Universal Life Insurance (IUL), the Swiss Army knife of financial planning. It's not just about protection; it's about growth, tax benefits, and being your financial BFF. As Benjamin Graham wisely said, "The individual investor should act consistently as an investor and not as a speculator." IUL is built on that principle, offering a balanced approach that "buy term and invest the difference" can't match.

The Verdict of Research

Financial brainiac Wade Pfau has done the homework. His research shows that IUL often outshines the old "invest the difference" strategy. IUL isn't just a death benefit—it's a tax-advantaged growth machine, potentially giving you better returns and more security.

The Practical Hurdles

Let's face it, human emotions and life's curveballs often derail the best-laid plans. The discipline to invest that extra cash? It's usually the first thing to go. Most Americans simply don't invest the difference—they spend it. And that, my friends, is where the whole strategy crumbles.

The Fallacy of 'Buy Term and Invest the Difference'

While the mantra has its charm, it doesn't address the nitty-gritty of real life. It assumes you'll invest those savings diligently, but life has a knack for throwing wrenches into our financial gears. Term insurance also leaves you vulnerable as you age, with skyrocketing premiums or lost coverage just when you need it most.

Indexed Universal Life Insurance: A Modern Solution

So, what makes IUL the superhero of modern finance? It's simple: lifelong coverage, tax advantages, and serious growth potential. Here's how IUL knocks out the competition:

Lifelong Coverage

Unlike term insurance, IUL sticks with you for life, ensuring your loved ones are always protected. No more worrying about outliving your coverage or getting slapped with sky-high premiums in your golden years.

Estate Planning and Wealth Transfer

IUL is a rockstar for estate planning. The death benefit is tax-free, making it a sleek way to transfer wealth. Plus, it can be structured to minimize estate taxes, keeping more of your hard-earned cash with your heirs.

Providing Generational Wealth While Living

Need funds for big life events? IUL lets you borrow against the cash value tax-free. Think of it like a financial Swiss Army knife, ready for anything from your kids' college tuition to starting a business. It's all about supporting your family without draining your retirement funds.

Example: My Personal Experience

I've got several IUL policies myself, creating a solid financial safety net for my family. These policies will help fund my daughter Brielle's education and other milestones, all while keeping my retirement savings intact. It's a win-win.

Transferring Wealth to Future Generations

When you pass, the IUL's death benefit goes to your beneficiaries tax-free. This can be a game-changer, helping them cover expenses, pay off debts, or invest. It's about leaving a legacy, not just a lump sum.

Example: My Estate Planning

I've set up a trust to ensure Brielle inherits assets at specific ages, with the IUL death benefits providing a substantial, tax-free inheritance. Despite not coming from wealth, we've structured our plan so Brielle will be a millionaire trust fund baby. This approach secures her financial future and preserves wealth for generations.

Conclusion

Indexed Universal Life Insurance smashes the limitations of old-school strategies like "Buy Term and Invest the Difference." With lifelong coverage, tax perks, and wealth-building potential, IUL is the powerhouse tool you need for modern financial planning. Ready to shake up your financial game? Let's dive into the next chapter and see why challenging the status quo with IUL could be the smartest move you ever make.

Next up, we're taking a critical look at the beloved 529 plans. Are they really the best option for funding your children's education, or is it time to toss them aside? In the upcoming chapter, we'll explore why Indexed Universal Life Insurance might just be the superior strategy for securing your kids' future and your own financial peace of mind. Get ready to challenge the status quo once again!

Chapter 6: Toss Your Kiddo's 529 Plan

Want the Best for Your Kids? Let's Talk 529 vs. IUL

We all want our kids to have what we didn't, right? The best schools, more money, a brighter future. If you're saving for your child's education, you're already a rockstar. But if you're considering a 529 plan, stop right there! You might be setting your kiddo up for a financial trap. Let's break it down and see why an Indexed Universal Life Insurance (IUL) policy might be the better choice for your child's future.

History and Mechanics of the 529 Plan

The 529 plan, born from Section 529 of the Internal Revenue Code in 1996, was designed to help families save for education with some sweet tax advantages. States, state agencies, and educational institutions sponsor these plans. There are two types: prepaid tuition plans and education savings plans.

How 529 Plans Work

You put in after-tax dollars, and the investments grow tax-deferred. When you withdraw money for qualified educational expenses, it's tax-free. There are no income limits for contributors, and you can contribute a ton — usually over $300,000.

Pros of 529 Plans

1. **Tax Advantages**: Earnings grow tax-deferred, and qualified withdrawals are tax-free.

2. **High Contribution Limits**: You can sock away a lot more than you can in a typical retirement account.

3. **State Tax Deductions**: Many states give you a tax break for contributions.

4. **Donor Control**: You stay in control of the funds and can change beneficiaries.

5. **Financial Aid Treatment**: Only a small percentage (up to 5.64%) of the 529's value counts against you in financial aid calculations.

Cons of 529 Plans

Despite the perks, 529 plans have some serious downsides:

1. **Limited Use**: Must be used for qualified education expenses, or else you face a 10% penalty plus income tax on earnings.

2. **Market Risk**: Investments can lose value in a bad market.

3.   **Financial Aid Impact**: Any amount considered can still ding your financial aid.

4.   **Investment Restrictions**: Limited to the plan's options, which can curb growth.

5.   **Estate Planning Limitations**: Transferring to another beneficiary can be a pain and subject to rules.

Why IUL is a Better Option for Our Kiddos

Now, let's explore why an IUL might be the superhero in your child's financial story.

Flexibility: Beyond Education

Unlike 529 plans, IUL policies are super flexible. You can access the cash value through tax-free loans for anything — starting a business, supplementing retirement income, covering unexpected expenses. If your child doesn't go to college, no big deal. No penalties, no taxes.

Tax Benefits: More Versatile

IULs work like Roth accounts with after-tax contributions and tax-deferred growth. But here's the kicker: you can pull out the money tax-free anytime for anything, thanks to policy loans. This makes IUL a powerful tool for handling unexpected financial needs.

Early Advantage: Cost and Compounding

One of the best reasons to get an IUL early is the lower cost. Life insurance is cheaper when you're young, meaning lower premiums and more time for the cash value to grow through compounding interest. My daughter Brielle has two IUL policies, and with our contributions, she'll be a millionaire before she hits 45. Talk about setting her up for success!

Impact on Financial Aid: Maximizing Support

IUL cash value isn't counted in FAFSA calculations, giving you a leg up on financial aid. Meanwhile, 529 plans can reduce the aid you get. Who needs that headache?

Risk Management: Protecting Your Investment

529 plans are tied to the market, which means they can lose value. IULs, however, have a floor that prevents the cash value from dropping due to market downturns. It's like having a financial safety net.

Long-Term Benefits: Beyond Education

529 plans are great until the education phase is over. Any leftover funds face penalties and taxes if not used for qualified expenses. IUL policies, however, keep growing and providing benefits throughout life. The cash value can be used for various needs, and the death benefit offers financial security for your heirs.

Estate Planning: A Legacy for the Future

IUL policies make estate planning easy. The death benefit passes to heirs tax-free, ensuring your financial legacy is preserved. 529 plans? Transferring to another beneficiary is cumbersome and subject to strict rules.

Case Studies: Real-Life Applications

The Smith Family

The Smiths invested in a 529 plan for their son. When he chose a non-traditional education path, they faced penalties and taxes on withdrawals. Their friends, the Johnsons, used an IUL policy. When their daughter started a business instead of attending college, they accessed the IUL's cash value tax-free, supporting her dreams without financial penalties.

The Williams Family

The Williams family enjoyed significant growth in their 529 plan during a bull market. But when the market crashed just as their child was ready for college, their account value plummeted. The Browns, with their IUL policy, saw their cash value remain stable due to the policy's market floor, ensuring funds were available when needed.

Conclusion: Making the Informed Choice

529 plans and IULs both offer benefits for funding education, but IULs shine with flexibility, risk management, long-term utility, and estate planning advantages. By weighing these factors, you can make a more informed decision that aligns with your financial goals and provides a robust foundation for your child's future.

When planning for your child's education, it's crucial to consider all options and consult with a financial advisor. The right strategy will secure a brighter financial future for your kids, free from the limitations and risks of traditional 529 plans.

Ready to flip the script on education savings? Let's dive into why Indexed Universal Life Insurance might be your new best friend in the next chapter. Buckle up, because we're about to revolutionize the way you think about saving for your child's future!

Chapter 7: Infinite Banking: Mastering Financial Freedom

Who WOULDN'T Want to Be Their Own Bank?

Seriously, who wouldn't want to be their own bank? Apparently, the "Buy Term & Invest The Difference" crowd is missing out. Infinite Banking is all about understanding and leveraging a financial strategy that's been hiding in plain sight, using Indexed Universal Life (IUL) policies to create your own personal banking system.

The Rise of "Infinite Banking"

Infinite Banking is gaining traction among those looking for true financial autonomy. This strategy turns permanent life insurance, especially IUL policies, into a powerhouse for financial empowerment. It's about taking control and making your money work for you in ways traditional banks can't.

What is Infinite Banking?

Infinite Banking uses IUL policies as your personal banking system. These policies build cash value over time, offering a financial cushion that you can borrow against whenever you need. It's like having a money tree in your backyard—but without the hassle of watering it.

The Mechanics of Infinite Banking

Infinite Banking isn't a product; it's a process. Once your IUL policy has built up enough cash value, you can borrow against it, using the policy as collateral. It's that simple—and that powerful. Think of it as a financial superpower that lets you tap into your own funds whenever you need them, no bank approval required.

Advantages Over Traditional Banking

1. **Direct Access to Funds**: Need money fast? Infinite Banking offers quicker liquidity compared to traditional loans.

2. **Flexible Repayments**: Repay on your own terms without the rigid schedules of conventional lenders. It's like having a loan from your favorite uncle who doesn't nag you about repayment.

3. **Enhanced Financial Control and Growth**: Gain direct control over your assets with higher growth potential, all wrapped in the security of life insurance. It's like having your cake and eating it too.

4. **Tax Benefits**: Enjoy tax efficiencies that traditional financial tools just can't match. It's like having a secret weapon in your financial arsenal.

Charting Your Course with Infinite Banking

Embarking on the Infinite Banking journey requires research, a solid financial assessment, and professional guidance. It's not a one-size-fits-all strategy, but when aligned with your financial goals, it's a game-changer. So, put on your captain's hat and get ready to navigate your way to financial freedom.

Understanding the Infinite Banking System

Infinite Banking leverages IUL policies to function as personalized financial ecosystems. These policies combine life coverage with cash value accumulation, letting you harness your savings dynamically. It's like turning your savings account into a Swiss Army knife of financial tools.

Accumulation and Borrowing Dynamics

One major perk of using IUL policies is the uninterrupted compounding of the cash value. Even when you borrow against your IUL, the cash value keeps growing as if the loan doesn't exist. This ensures your growth trajectory remains strong. It's like having your money work overtime without demanding extra pay.

Interest Rates and Loan Flexibility

Borrowing against an IUL policy typically means lower interest rates than traditional loans. Plus, the repayment terms are highly flexible, allowing you to repay loans at your convenience. Imagine borrowing money without the bank breathing down your neck—it's liberating.

Tax Efficiency and Wealth Protection

IULs offer tax-deferred growth of cash value and policy loans aren't considered taxable income. This is a significant advantage for wealth management and retirement planning. It's like having a financial shield protecting your money from the taxman.

The Role of Social Media in Promoting Infinite Banking

Social media has been a game-changer for Infinite Banking over the past decade. Platforms like YouTube, Instagram, and financial blogs have become hubs for sharing success stories, educational content, and detailed guides, making Infinite Banking more accessible than ever. Influencers and financial advisors use these platforms to demystify the strategy, contributing to its rapid adoption.

The Social Media Boom

Over the past 10 years, social media has revolutionized how financial concepts are shared and understood. Infinite Banking has particularly benefited from this shift, as complex financial strategies can now be explained in engaging, easy-to-understand formats. Financial gurus and everyday users alike post videos, infographics, and testimonials that highlight the benefits and practical applications of Infinite Banking. It's like having a financial advisor in your pocket.

Influencer Impact

Influencers play a crucial role in promoting Infinite Banking. By sharing their personal success stories and breaking down the strategy into bite-sized content, they make the concept approachable and relatable. This has led to a surge in interest and adoption, as more people realize the potential of becoming their own bank. Influencers are like the cool kids who make everyone else want to join the Infinite Banking club.

Community Building

Social media platforms also foster communities where users can share experiences, ask questions, and offer advice. These communities provide support and build confidence among those considering Infinite Banking. The collective knowledge and real-life examples shared in these groups further drive the popularity and understanding of the strategy. It's like having a support group for your financial goals.

Ensuring Proper Structure for Maximum Cash Value Accumulation

For families looking to adopt Infinite Banking, it's crucial to set up the banking structure correctly to maximize cash value accumulation. Here's how:

1. **Choosing the Right Policy**: Select an IUL policy that aligns with your long-term goals.

2. **Optimizing Premium Payments**: Fund the policy strategically to accelerate cash value growth.

3. **Regular Monitoring and Adjustments**: Periodically review the policy performance and adjust as needed.

4. **Professional Guidance****: Work with financial advisors specializing in Infinite Banking to tailor the strategy to your situation.

Practical Applications of Infinite Banking

1.   **Business Financing**: Entrepreneurs can use their policy's cash value to fund business ventures, bypassing traditional financing methods. It's like having a business partner who never asks for equity.

2.   **Real Estate Investments**: Borrow against your IUL to invest in real estate, leveraging the policy's value to grow your investment portfolio. It's like having a magic wand for your real estate dreams.

3.   **Emergency Fund**: Use the cash value as an accessible emergency fund, providing liquidity without having to liquidate other investments. It's like having a rainy day fund that never runs dry.

Case Studies and Success Stories

Real-Life Examples

1.   **Entrepreneurial Success**: John used his IUL policy's cash value to fund a startup, avoiding the high-interest rates of bank loans. His business thrived, and he repaid the policy loan on his terms. It's like having a secret stash of money that you can tap into when the banks slam their doors.

2.   **Real Estate Expansion**: Maria leveraged her IUL policy to invest in rental properties. Using the policy's cash value, she secured prime real estate, generating rental income and growing her wealth. It's like turning your life insurance into a real estate goldmine.

Conclusion

Infinite Banking, especially when paired with IUL, offers a tantalizing solution to financial anxiety. It promises not just growth and security, but also unparalleled control over your finances. But remember, this journey requires caution, knowledge, and wisdom. As investment guru Peter Lynch said, "Know what you own, and know why you own it." With this mindset, you're well on your way to financial autonomy and a promising horizon.

But hold on, not everyone is on board with Infinite Banking and IULs. You've probably heard some of the grumbling: "It's too complicated," "It's not worth it," or "Just buy term and invest the difference." These misconceptions can deter people from exploring the true benefits of IUL.

In the next chapter, we're going to dive deep into these myths and misconceptions. We'll debunk the most common criticisms and show you why IUL is not only a viable option but often the superior choice. Get ready to challenge the status quo and see why IUL deserves a spot in your financial strategy. Buckle up as we set the record straight and shine a light on the truth behind Indexed Universal Life Insurance in Chapter 8: What the IUL Haters Say, Debunking the Myths lingering out there.

Chapter 8: What the IUL Haters Say

Introduction

As awesome as IUL is, it isn't without its fair share of haters. Despite the numerous benefits of Indexed Universal Life Insurance (IUL), it faces considerable criticism from financial experts and advisors who advocate for more traditional financial products. Understanding these criticisms and the realities behind them is essential for making informed decisions. This chapter will address and debunk some of the most common myths about IUL, reinforcing its benefits and highlighting its unique advantages.

Common Myths and Criticisms

Myth 1: Complexity and Lack of Understanding

Criticism: One of the primary criticisms of IUL is its complexity. Critics argue that IUL policies are difficult to understand and manage, making them unsuitable for the average consumer.

Reality: While IUL policies can be complex, proper education and guidance can make these complexities manageable. Working with a knowledgeable advisor can help demystify these products and ensure you are leveraging their benefits effectively. Once you grasp the basic concepts, an IUL is no more complicated than other financial products, like mutual funds or 401(k) plans. It's a tool that, when properly structured, can create significant wealth through tax-advantaged growth and protection features.

Myth 2: High Fees and Costs

Criticism: Another common criticism is the perceived high fees and costs associated with IUL policies. Critics argue that these fees can erode the cash value and reduce the overall benefits of the policy.

Reality: While IUL policies may have higher upfront costs compared to term life insurance, these fees cover added benefits and protections, such as lifetime coverage, living benefits, and cash value accumulation. Over time, the growth potential and tax advantages of IUL can offset these initial costs. It's important to consider the long-term benefits, not just the upfront costs, when evaluating IUL policies. Additionally, the costs associated with IUL are often less than those of actively managed mutual funds, which many people invest in without hesitation.

Myth 3: Market Performance and Caps

Criticism: Critics argue that the growth of the cash value in an IUL policy is capped, meaning that during years of exceptional market performance, policyholders may not fully benefit from the market's gains.

Reality: FALSE. While earlier renditions did have a cap, these days, many IULs don't have caps. The ceiling has been removed from your earning potential! Even when caps are present, they are balanced by the policy's protection against market losses, ensuring that the cash value does not decrease during market downturns.

Myth 4: Comparisons to Buy Term and Invest the Difference

Criticism: The "Buy Term and Invest the Difference" strategy suggests purchasing term life insurance and investing the premium savings in the stock market. Critics argue that this strategy provides better returns and more flexibility than IUL.

Reality: While "Buy Term and Invest the Difference" can be effective for disciplined investors, it does not offer the same tax advantages, lifetime coverage, or protection against market downturns that IUL provides. Many individuals lack the discipline required to consistently invest the difference. Additionally, the tax-deferred growth and tax-free loans available through IUL policies offer significant benefits not available with term life insurance and traditional investments. Moreover, term life insurance policies expire, often leaving policyholders without coverage at an age when they need it most. And as long said before, people usually don't save the damn difference.

Myth 5: Poor Historical Performance

Criticism: Some critics argue that IULs have historically underperformed compared to other investment options, such as mutual funds or stocks.

Reality: MALARKEY! While the historical performance of IULs may not always match the highest-performing mutual funds or stocks during bull markets, IULs provide a balance of growth potential and protection against market downturns. The average returns of IULs over time have been competitive, especially when considering their downside protection. This means that even in volatile markets, your cash value is safeguarded against losses, making IULs a stable option for long-term financial planning. So it's not so much about how much you earn, but how much you can keep.

Myth 6: Limited Investment Options

Criticism: Critics claim that IUL policies offer limited investment choices compared to other investment vehicles.

Reality: Dude, what?! IULs are linked to specific market indexes but offer a variety of crediting strategies that allow for tailored growth opportunities based on your financial goals and risk tolerance. These strategies can be adjusted over time, offering more flexibility than often acknowledged. Additionally, the indices used in IULs are typically well-established and diversified, providing broad market exposure without the risks associated with more volatile or narrowly focused investments.

Myth 7: Policy Loans and Interest Rates

Criticism: Some argue that policy loans from an IUL are disadvantageous due to interest charges that could offset the benefits.

Reality: Policy loans from IULs offer significant advantages, including tax-free access to the cash value. While loans accrue interest, the net effect can still be highly favorable, especially compared to traditional loans or early withdrawals from other investment accounts that may incur taxes and penalties. The interest rate on these loans is often lower than rates on personal loans or credit cards, making them a cost-effective option for accessing liquidity when needed. Properly managed, the interest on the loan can be offset by the policy's continued growth.

Myth 8: Misleading Illustrations

Criticism: There is a concern that the illustrations used to sell IULs can be misleading, projecting overly optimistic returns.

Reality: No no no. It's essential to scrutinize the assumptions behind any financial illustration. Ethical advisors present realistic scenarios, including both optimistic and conservative projections, to give a balanced view. While projections can vary, the underlying benefits of tax-deferred growth, market protection, and flexible premium payments remain robust. When choosing an IUL, working with a reputable advisor who can provide transparent and realistic illustrations is crucial. I along with my advisors always promise to underpromise and overdeliver.

Myth 9: Suitability for the Average Investor

Criticism: Some argue that IULs are only suitable for high-net-worth individuals and not for the average investor.

Reality: Stop it! While IULs are popular among high-net-worth individuals due to their tax advantages and wealth preservation features, they can also be highly beneficial for average investors. The flexibility of premium payments and the ability to adjust coverage make IULs accessible and adaptable to various financial situations. Average investors can use IULs to build wealth, protect their families, and secure their financial future with the added benefits of lifetime coverage and potential tax-free retirement income.

Why Financial Advisors Often Don't Recommend IUL

Many financial advisors do not recommend IUL policies, and there are several reasons for this:

1. **Licensing and Knowledge**: Not all financial advisors are licensed to sell life insurance

products, including IUL. This lack of licensing and knowledge about these products leads to a preference for traditional investment products that they are more familiar with.

2.   **Compensation Structure**: Financial advisors typically earn commissions based on assets under management (AUM). This means they are incentivized to keep your money in investment products that generate ongoing fees, such as mutual funds and managed accounts. They don't earn commissions from IUL policies, which can lead to a bias against recommending them. Advisors still make money on your investments, regardless of whether you make money or not. They earn their fees based on the total assets they manage, which means they have a vested interest in keeping your money in traditional investments like mutual funds and variable funds where they can charge ongoing fees.

Embracing Change: Overcoming Fear of the Unknown

The financial strategies of the 1950s, 60s, and 70s are deeply ingrained in our collective consciousness. These decades shaped how many people view financial security, primarily through pensions and straightforward savings plans. However, the financial landscape has evolved, and so must our strategies.

People often fear change because it represents the unknown. This fear is understandable but can be detrimental. Michael Jordan, one of the greatest basketball players of all time, was initially feared and misunderstood because he did things no one had seen before. He broke the mold and redefined what was possible. Similarly, IUL is a modern financial tool that breaks the mold of traditional financial planning. Just as Jordan's revolutionary approach to basketball changed the game, embracing new financial strategies like IUL can revolutionize your financial future.

The Simplicity and Power of IUL

Despite the myths and criticisms, the core concept of IUL is simple and powerful: it combines life insurance with an investment component that grows based on the performance of a market index, offering both protection and growth potential. Here's how it can create wealth:

1. **Tax-Deferred Growth**: Your cash value grows without being taxed, allowing it to compound more effectively.

2. **Tax-Free Loans**: Accessing the cash value through loans means you can use your money without incurring taxes.

3. **Market Protection**: With a guaranteed minimum interest rate, your investment is protected from market losses.

4. **Flexible Premiums**: Adjust your premium payments based on your financial situation, ensuring the policy remains affordable.

5. **Lifetime Coverage**: Unlike term life insurance, an IUL policy provides coverage for life, ensuring your loved ones are protected no matter what.

6. **Living Benefits**: Many IUL policies include living benefits that provide access to funds in case of

critical, chronic, or terminal illness, adding an extra layer of financial security that traditional term policies typically do not offer.

Conclusion

Indexed Universal Life Insurance (IUL) faces its fair share of criticism due to its complexity, perceived high costs, and supposed limitations. However, these criticisms often stem from misunderstandings or a focus on short-term gains. By educating yourself about the realities of IUL and working with knowledgeable advisors, you can make informed decisions that align with your long-term financial goals. Embracing IUL can provide you with a powerful tool for building and preserving wealth, offering benefits that extend far beyond those of traditional financial products.

Don't let fear of the unknown or outdated thinking prevent you from exploring innovative financial strategies that can secure your future. To all the naysayers, it's time to stop the hating and start understanding the true potential of IUL.

Next up, we're shifting gears to focus on the importance of planning and avoiding common pitfalls. Financial success doesn't just happen; it's crafted with careful planning and strategic decisions. Ready to learn how to steer clear of the mistakes that can derail your financial future? Buckle up for Chapter 8. We'll dive into the essential elements of effective planning and how to dodge the most common pitfalls on your path to financial freedom.

Chapter 9: You Only Fail When You Fail to Plan

Introduction

Navigating the financial landscape can feel like trying to cross a minefield blindfolded. One wrong step and BOOM – there goes your financial security. Understanding common pitfalls and how to avoid them is crucial for achieving financial stability and growth. This chapter will delve into some of the most prevalent financial mistakes people make and provide strategies to circumvent them, ensuring a smoother path toward financial success.

The Biggest Financial Mistakes

1. Not Starting Early Enough

One of the biggest mistakes people make is delaying their saving and investing efforts. The power of compounding interest means that the earlier you start, the more your money can grow over time. Robert Kiyosaki nails it when he says, "The biggest financial mistake people make is to not start saving and investing early." Starting early gives your investments more time to grow and recover from market fluctuations.

Strategy: Start Small but Start Now

Even if you can only afford to set aside a small amount each month, the key is to start now. Over time, these small contributions can add up significantly. Utilize automatic transfers to a savings or investment account to ensure consistency. Just do it – your future self will thank you.

2. Failing to Diversify Investments

Putting all your eggs in one basket is a recipe for disaster. Market conditions can change faster than you can say "stock market crash," and having a diversified portfolio can help mitigate risks. Diversification involves spreading investments across different asset classes, such as stocks, bonds, real estate, and more.

Strategy: Diversify Your Portfolio

Work with a financial advisor to create a diversified investment portfolio that aligns with your risk tolerance and financial goals. Consider including Indexed Universal Life Insurance (IUL) as part of your diversified strategy, as it offers tax advantages and protection against market downturns.

3. Ignoring Inflation

Inflation is the silent killer of your purchasing power. Many people underestimate the impact of inflation on their long-term financial goals, leading to insufficient savings for retirement and other future needs.

Strategy: Invest in Inflation-Protected Assets

Consider investments that offer protection against inflation, such as Treasury Inflation-Protected Securities (TIPS) and real estate. Additionally, the cash value growth in an IUL policy can help hedge against inflation, ensuring your savings retain their value over time.

4. Overlooking the Importance of Tax Planning

Taxes can take a huge bite out of your financial outcomes. Failing to incorporate tax planning into your financial strategy can result in higher tax liabilities and reduced wealth accumulation.

Strategy: Utilize Tax-Advantaged Accounts

Make use of tax-advantaged accounts such as Roth IRAs, 401(k)s, and IUL policies. These accounts offer various tax benefits, such as tax-deferred growth and tax-free withdrawals, which can enhance your long-term financial security.

5. Lack of Financial Literacy

Many financial mistakes stem from a lack of understanding of basic financial principles. Without adequate financial literacy, individuals are more likely to make poor investment decisions, fall into debt, and fail to plan adequately for the future.

Strategy: Invest in Financial Education

Continuously educate yourself about personal finance. Books by financial experts like Tony Robbins, Robert Kiyosaki, and David McKnight provide valuable insights and strategies for managing your finances effectively. Attend workshops, seminars, and online courses to deepen your financial knowledge.

The Role of Indexed Universal Life Insurance (IUL) in Avoiding Pitfalls

IUL policies can play a significant role in helping you avoid common financial pitfalls. Here's how:

1. Starting Early with IUL

By investing in an IUL policy early, you take advantage of compounding interest and tax-deferred growth. This early start can significantly enhance your long-term financial security.

2. Diversification with IUL

Including an IUL policy in your financial plan adds a layer of diversification. The policy's cash value grows based on a stock market index, but with a protective floor that shields against market losses, offering a balanced approach to growth and security.

3. Hedging Against Inflation with IUL

The cash value in an IUL policy can grow at a rate that outpaces inflation, helping to preserve the purchasing power of your savings. This makes IUL an effective tool for long-term wealth preservation.

4. Tax Planning with IUL

IUL offers significant tax advantages, such as tax-deferred growth of the cash value and tax-free loans. These benefits can reduce your overall tax burden and enhance your wealth accumulation efforts.

5. Enhancing Financial Literacy

Working with a financial advisor to understand the complexities of IUL policies can improve your financial literacy. Advisors can help you make informed decisions and integrate IUL into a comprehensive financial plan that aligns with your goals.

Real-Life Success Stories

Case Study: Sarah's Financial Transformation

Sarah, a 35-year-old professional, realized she was not saving enough for retirement. After consulting with a financial advisor, she decided to invest in an IUL policy. By starting early and making consistent contributions, Sarah watched her cash value grow significantly over the years. The tax-deferred growth and tax-free loans allowed her to fund her children's education and cover unexpected expenses without dipping into her retirement savings.

Case Study: Mike's Diversification Strategy

Mike, a 50-year-old entrepreneur, had most of his investments in the stock market. Recognizing the need for diversification, he included an IUL policy in his portfolio. The policy's growth potential, combined with its protective floor, provided Mike with a balanced approach to wealth accumulation. When the market experienced a downturn, Mike's IUL policy safeguarded his savings, demonstrating the importance of diversification.

Conclusion

Avoiding common financial pitfalls requires proactive planning, education, and strategic use of financial tools like Indexed Universal Life Insurance (IUL). By starting early, diversifying investments, planning for inflation, incorporating tax strategies, and continuously improving financial literacy, you can build a robust financial foundation. Embracing these strategies will help you navigate the complexities of the financial landscape, achieve your long-term goals, and secure a prosperous future.

Remember, failing to plan is planning to fail. So, arm yourself with knowledge, stay disciplined, and make informed decisions to avoid the common financial traps. In the next chapter, we'll dive into how to navigate the tricky waters of financial planning for high-net-worth individuals and explore how to use IUL to manage substantial incomes, preserve wealth, and plan for retirement. Stay tuned!

Chapter 10: Legends and Legacies: Titans of Life Insurance

Introduction

The wealthy have long understood the power of life insurance as a tool for building and preserving wealth across generations. By examining the strategies employed by financial titans, we can uncover the transformative potential of Indexed Universal Life Insurance (IUL) in creating lasting legacies.

The Importance of Legacy

Andrew Carnegie once said, "The man who dies...rich dies disgraced." This sentiment underscores the importance of not only accumulating wealth but also using it to benefit future generations. Life insurance, particularly IUL, offers a powerful means to achieve this goal. Through prudent use of life insurance, individuals can ensure their wealth not only provides for their descendants but also fosters philanthropic initiatives and societal contributions that resonate for years to come.

Strategies of Financial Titans

Case Study: John D. Rockefeller

John D. Rockefeller, one of the wealthiest individuals in history, was a pioneer in using life insurance to secure his family's financial future. Rockefeller understood that life insurance could provide a stable foundation for wealth preservation and transfer. He utilized cash value life insurance policies to ensure that his descendants would inherit not only his fortune but also the values and principles he held dear.

Rockefeller's legacy is a testament to his strategic use of life insurance. By planning meticulously and using life insurance as a key component of his estate, he could create a financial safety net that protected his family's wealth from the erosive effects of taxes and market volatility. This foresight ensured that the Rockefeller name remained synonymous with wealth and philanthropy for generations.

Beyond financial planning, Rockefeller also used his life insurance policies to fund various charitable endeavors. He believed in the principle of stewardship and used his wealth to support causes such as education, public health, and scientific research. His establishment of the Rockefeller Foundation, funded partly through life insurance, showcases how life insurance can be leveraged to support philanthropic goals, creating a legacy that extends beyond financial wealth.

Key Takeaways:

- **Wealth Preservation**: Life insurance helps maintain wealth across generations.

- **Estate Planning**: Strategic use of life insurance can minimize tax liabilities.

Case Study: Walt Disney

Walt Disney, the creator and genius behind all things Disney and Marvel today, used the cash value from his life insurance policy to fund the creation of Disneyland. When traditional banks told him to get lost, Disney turned to his life insurance. This strategic use of life insurance allowed Disney to realize his vision and create a legacy that continues to impact the world today. If only the banks had listened, right? Missed opportunity!

Disney's foresight in leveraging life insurance exemplifies how financial tools can be used innovatively to fuel large-scale ventures that outlast their creators. The cash value of his life insurance policy provided Disney with the necessary capital when traditional funding sources were unavailable or reluctant to invest in his dream.

Key Takeaways:

- **Vision Realization**: Life insurance can be a source of capital for groundbreaking projects.

- **Legacy Building**: Strategic financial planning ensures enduring impacts beyond one's lifetime.

- **Financial Creativity**: Leveraging life insurance can overcome traditional financial barriers.

Case Study: Ray Kroc

Ray Kroc, the man who made McDonald's a global empire, also tapped into life insurance. By using the cash value of his policies, Kroc expanded his business, navigated financial challenges, and seized opportunities. His story highlights life insurance as a versatile financial tool for business growth.

Kroc's use of life insurance ensured McDonald's could weather economic downturns and continue growing. It also played a critical role in his estate planning, securing wealth for his heirs and minimizing their tax burden.

Key Takeaways:

- **Business Expansion**: Life insurance can provide essential funding for business growth.

- **Financial Stability**: Access to cash value in policies can offer financial security during expansion phases.

- **Versatility**: Life insurance supports entrepreneurial ventures and long-term business success.

Case Study: Jim Harbaugh

Former Michigan head coach Jim Harbaugh had an Indexed Universal Life Insurance (IUL) policy structured into his contract with the University of Michigan. This innovative arrangement provided him with tax-free earnings, demonstrating a modern application of IUL in personal financial planning. According to a Forbes article, Harbaugh's contract included annual premium payments made by the university, enhancing his financial stability and future wealth accumulation.

Harbaugh's use of an IUL policy in his compensation package exemplifies a forward-thinking approach to financial planning. By integrating life insurance into his contract, Harbaugh ensured that he would have a secure financial future with significant tax advantages. This arrangement not only provided him with peace of mind but also served as a model for other professionals seeking innovative ways to structure their compensation for long-term benefits.

Key Takeaways:

- **Tax-Free Earnings**: Structuring IUL policies into compensation packages can provide significant tax advantages.

- **Innovative Compensation**: Leveraging life insurance in employment contracts can offer long-term financial benefits.

Case Study: Dabo Swinney

Dabo Swinney, the celebrated head football coach at Clemson University, has also utilized cash value life insurance as part of his compensation package. Swinney's contract includes a split-dollar life insurance agreement, where the university pays the premiums and, in return, receives a portion of the cash value and death benefit. This structure not only provides Swinney with significant financial benefits but also serves as an innovative tool for Clemson to retain one of the most successful coaches in college football.

Swinney's use of life insurance illustrates the creative ways in which high-profile individuals can leverage these policies for both personal and professional benefit. The split-dollar arrangement offers tax advantages and financial flexibility, making it an attractive option for coaches and executives alike.

Key Takeaways:

- **Employee Retention**: Life insurance can be a valuable tool for retaining top talent.

- **Financial Security**: Split-dollar arrangements offer financial benefits and flexibility.

- **Innovative Compensation**: Incorporating life insurance into contracts can provide significant advantages.

Case Study: Dawn Staley

Dawn Staley, the head coach and NCAA Women's Basketball Champion of the South Carolina women's basketball team, has also leveraged life insurance as part of her comprehensive financial strategy. Recognizing the importance of financial security and long-term planning, Staley's contract includes a significant life insurance component. This not only provides her with a robust financial safety net but also ensures that her contributions to the sport and her legacy are well-protected.

Staley's use of life insurance is part of a broader trend among high-profile coaches to secure their financial futures through innovative compensation packages. The life insurance policies included in her contract are designed to accumulate cash value over time, offering Staley the flexibility to access funds for personal or professional needs.

Key Takeaways:

- **Financial Flexibility**: Life insurance policies offer access to funds for various needs.

- **Long-Term Security**: Strategic use of life insurance ensures financial stability.

- **Role Model**: Staley's approach serves as an inspiration for other professionals.

Case Study: Brian Kelly

Brian Kelly, head football coach at LSU, has similarly utilized life insurance as a strategic component of his financial planning. Kelly's contract includes a split-dollar life insurance agreement, reflecting a growing trend among high-profile coaches to leverage these policies for both financial security and estate planning purposes. The split-dollar arrangement allows LSU to pay the premiums while Kelly benefits from the accumulated cash value and death benefit.

Kelly's use of life insurance is a testament to the versatility and strategic benefits of these policies. By incorporating life insurance into his compensation package, Kelly ensures that he has a reliable source of funds for future needs, whether personal or professional.

Key Takeaways:

- **Customized Solutions**: Split-dollar arrangements can be tailored to meet specific needs.

- **Tax Advantages**: Strategic use of life insurance offers significant tax benefits.

- **Proactive Planning**: Leveraging life insurance ensures financial stability and security.

Modern Applications of IUL

Creating a Lasting Impact

Modern entrepreneurs and high-net-worth individuals use IUL policies to create lasting impacts. By funding charitable endeavors and establishing trusts, they ensure their wealth benefits future generations and causes they care about. IUL policies offer flexibility and growth potential, making them an attractive option for those looking to make a significant, enduring difference.

Key Takeaways:

- **Philanthropy**: IUL policies can be instrumental in funding charitable activities.

- **Wealth Preservation**: Establishing trusts with IUL ensures wealth is managed and distributed according to the policyholder's wishes.

Estate Planning and Wealth Transfer

IUL policies play a critical role in estate planning. The tax-free death benefit provides a seamless transfer of wealth, ensuring that heirs receive the maximum benefit without the burden of estate taxes. This aspect of IUL makes it an invaluable tool in preserving wealth across generations, maintaining family legacies, and preventing the dissipation of estates due to tax liabilities.

Key Takeaways:

- **Tax Efficiency**: IUL policies offer tax-free death benefits, enhancing wealth transfer.

- **Seamless Transfer**: Policies ensure heirs receive benefits without significant tax burdens.

Conclusion

Leveraging life insurance for legacy is a time-tested strategy employed by financial titans throughout history. By incorporating Indexed Universal Life Insurance (IUL) into their financial plans, individuals can create lasting legacies that benefit future generations and contribute to their enduring impact on the world. The stories of John D. Rockefeller, Walt Disney, Ray Kroc, Jim Harbaugh, Dabo Swinney, Dawn Staley, and Brian Kelly demonstrate the power of life insurance in realizing visions, expanding empires, and enhancing financial stability. Modern applications of IUL in estate planning and philanthropy further highlight its relevance and potential. Through strategic use of IUL, one can ensure their wealth serves a greater purpose, transcending their lifetime and continuing to make a positive impact for generations to come.

However, the benefits of IUL aren't just for historical figures or those in the public eye. High-net-worth individuals today are increasingly turning to IUL to manage their substantial incomes, preserve their wealth, plan for retirement, and efficiently transfer their assets. These strategies allow them to leverage IUL's unique advantages to secure their financial futures and build legacies that endure.

In the next chapter, we will explore how high-net-worth individuals utilize IUL to achieve these goals. We'll delve into real-world examples and strategies that demonstrate the flexibility and power of IUL for those with significant financial resources. Join us as we uncover the sophisticated financial tactics that make IUL an indispensable tool for the wealthy and see how you can apply these strategies to your own financial planning. Get ready to elevate your financial game and secure your legacy.

Chapter 11: Case Studies and Real-Life Success Stories

Introduction

Gather around, folks! Let's dive into the nitty-gritty of how real people — like you and me — have cracked the code of financial freedom with Indexed Universal Life Insurance (IUL). These stories aren't just tales from a glossy brochure; they're real-life transformations, full of lessons, laughs, and maybe a few happy tears. So grab your popcorn and get ready to be inspired by these financial superheroes.

Case Study 1: The Smith Family – Funding Education and Securing Retirement

Background

Meet John and Sarah Smith, your typical mid-40s couple juggling the demands of parenting and planning for retirement. With kids eyeing expensive college degrees and a nest egg that needed serious fluffing, they were feeling the squeeze.

Strategy

Enter the IUL policy, stage left. After a chat with their savvy financial advisor, the Smiths decided to invest in an IUL policy with flexible premiums. This wasn't just a plan; it was their financial Swiss Army knife. The advisor broke down how the cash value of the policy could grow tax-deferred and be tapped into tax-free through policy loans. Talk about a win-win!

Outcome

Fast forward ten years: the Smiths had beefed up their IUL policy like it was hitting the gym every day. When their eldest was ready for college, they borrowed against the policy's cash value, avoiding those dreaded student loans. Meanwhile, the policy kept growing, ensuring a comfy retirement cushion. No more sleepless nights — just solid financial peace of mind.

Case Study 2: Mike the Athlete – Managing Tax Liabilities and Ensuring Long-Term Stability

Background

Say hello to Mike, a professional basketball player with a bank account that soared and a career span that didn't. High earnings? Check. High taxes? Double check. Long-term financial stability? Not so much.

Strategy

Mike's financial guru recommended an IUL policy to tackle his two-headed monster of taxes and future security. This policy offered tax-deferred growth and tax-free loans, allowing Mike to grow his wealth without Uncle Sam taking a huge bite.

Outcome

Mike made the smart play and invested in an IUL policy, contributing a chunk of his earnings each year. Post-retirement, his policy's cash value had grown like a well-watered plant. He accessed funds tax-free, keeping his lifestyle plush. And the cherry on top? A death benefit ensuring his family was set. Slam dunk, Mike!

Case Study 3: Susan the Business Owner – Business Succession Planning and Wealth Transfer

Background

Meet Susan, a powerhouse business owner in her 50s. She wanted to make sure her business thrived even if she wasn't at the helm and wanted to pass on her wealth to her kids without a hitch.

Strategy

Susan's financial whiz suggested an IUL policy as the cornerstone of her business succession plan. This policy would ensure a smooth leadership transition and offer tax-free cash value for any business or personal needs.

Outcome

Susan committed to the IUL policy, and it paid off big time. The cash value grew, giving her business a safety net. When she retired, the death benefit facilitated the buyout of her shares, keeping the business steady. Plus, the tax-free loans gave her a sweet retirement income. Talk about retiring in style!

Case Study 4: David the Executive – Enhancing Compensation Packages and Retaining Talent

Background

David, an executive at a mid-sized company, was on a mission to attract and keep top-notch employees. He needed a compensation package that wowed without draining the company coffers.

Strategy

David's financial advisor had the perfect solution: IUL policies as part of an executive bonus plan. These policies offered life insurance protection and cash value growth, making them a hot ticket for employee satisfaction.

Outcome

David rolled out the IUL-based bonus plan, and it was a hit. The company attracted and retained star talent, performance soared, and employees were thrilled with the financial perks. The tax advantages and policy flexibility? Just the icing on the cake.

Lessons Learned

1. **Strategic Use of Policy Loans**: Loans against the cash value of an IUL policy can provide financial flexibility without the tax bite.

2. **Long-Term Planning**: IUL policies are the gift that keeps on giving, perfect for both immediate needs and future goals.

3. **Comprehensive Financial Solutions**: IULs can be woven into various strategies, from personal wealth management to business succession.

4. **Tax Efficiency**: The tax-deferred growth and tax-free access to funds make IUL a smart, tax-efficient choice for wealth management.

Conclusion

These case studies show the transformative power of Indexed Universal Life Insurance (IUL). From funding education and managing taxes to ensuring business continuity and enhancing compensation packages, IUL can be a game-changer. Now that we've seen how everyday heroes leverage IUL, let's turn the page and dive into how high-income earners use this financial tool to secure their fortunes and build lasting legacies. Buckle up; it's going to be an eye-opening ride!

Chapter 12: High Earners, Future Wealth Builders

In today's whirlwind world, many folks rake in a hefty income but still find their bank accounts lacking that sweet, sweet wealth. These people are often called High Earners, Future Wealth Builders. We're talking about professionals like doctors, lawyers, engineers, and corporate execs, typically aged 25 to 45, pulling in $100,000 to $250,000 a year. Despite their impressive paychecks, they're often bogged down by student debt, sky-high living costs, and a lifestyle that eats up most of their cash. This chapter digs into how Indexed Universal Life Insurance (IUL) can be the ultimate financial hack for Future Wealth Builders, helping them build and keep wealth for their future and their families.

The Financial Challenges of Future Wealth Builders

Meet Sarah and James, a power couple in their early 30s living in a bustling city. Sarah's a corporate attorney, and James is a software engineer, earning a combined $200,000 a year. On paper, they're rolling in it, but their financial reality tells a different story. They're dealing with:

- **Substantial Student Debt**: Together, they owe $150,000 in student loans, gobbling up a big chunk of their monthly income.

- **High Living Costs**: City living means expensive rent, steep transportation costs, and daily expenses that add up fast.

- **Lifestyle Inflation**: As their income grew, so did their spending on fancy dinners, vacations, and luxury items.

- **Lack of Savings**: Despite their earnings, they have little saved up, making them vulnerable to financial surprises.

Sarah and James, like many in their shoes, are stuck in a cycle of earning big but saving little. They need a strategy to make their income work harder for them, paving the way to a secure financial future.

The Power of Indexed Universal Life Insurance (IUL)

Indexed Universal Life Insurance (IUL) offers a powerful solution for Future Wealth Builders like Sarah and James. Here's how IUL can flip their financial script:

1.   **Dual Benefit**:

       ◦   **Protection**: IUL provides a death benefit that ensures Sarah and James's family is covered in case of an untimely death.

       ◦   **Wealth Accumulation**: The cash value component of an IUL grows based on the performance of an equity index like the S&P 500, offering the potential for significant growth without direct exposure to market risks.

2.   **Tax Advantages**:

       ◦   **Tax-Deferred Growth**: The cash value in an IUL policy grows tax-deferred, letting Sarah and James accumulate wealth more efficiently.

       ◦   **Tax-Free Loans and Withdrawals**: Policy loans and withdrawals can be taken out tax-free, providing a flexible source of funds for emergencies, retirement, or other needs.

3.   **Flexibility and Control**:

       ◦   **Premium Flexibility**: IUL policies allow for flexible premium payments, making it easier for Sarah and James to adjust their contributions based on their financial situation.

       ◦   **Adjustable Death Benefit**: They can increase or decrease the death benefit as their needs change over time.

Common Alternatives: Roth IRA and Employer-Matched 401(k)

Now, let's talk about the usual suspects in the world of retirement savings — the Roth IRA and the employer-matched 401(k). These are like the vanilla ice cream of retirement plans: reliable, predictable, but sometimes, you just want something with a little more kick.

1. **Roth IRA Limitations**:

    ◦ **Income Restrictions**: Roth IRAs have income limits that can prevent high earners from contributing. For single filers, the phase-out range begins at $129,000 and ends at $144,000, while for married couples filing jointly, it starts at $204,000 and ends at $214,000. So if you're making the big bucks, Uncle Sam might just say, "Sorry, not for you."

    ◦ **Contribution Limits**: The maximum annual contribution to a Roth IRA is $6,000 ($7,000 if you're age 50 or older), which might cover a few Netflix subscriptions but won't get you a yacht anytime soon.

2. **401(k) Plan Limitations**:

    ◦ **Market Volatility**: Both Roth IRAs and 401(k) plans are subject to market volatility. When the market dips, your retirement savings can feel like they're on a roller coaster, and not the fun kind.

    ◦ **Contribution Limits**: While 401(k) plans have higher contribution limits ($20,500 for individuals under 50, with an additional $6,500 catch-up contribution for those 50 and older), these limits can still be restrictive if you're looking to stash away some serious cash for your golden years.

Why IUL is a Superior Choice

Stop Spending, Start Saving: Future Wealth Builders often find themselves in a spending cycle due to their high income and societal pressures. An IUL policy encourages disciplined saving by requiring regular premium payments. These payments not only build the cash value but also ensure long-term financial protection.

Market Protection with Growth Potential: Unlike Roth IRAs and 401(k) plans, IUL policies offer protection against market downturns. The cash value grows based on the performance of an equity index, but with a guaranteed minimum interest rate, ensuring that your savings are protected even in volatile markets.

Building a Financial Legacy: For Future Wealth Builders looking to build a lasting legacy, IUL offers an effective tool. The death benefit can provide significant financial support to their heirs, while the accumulated cash value can be used for various needs, including education funding and retirement.

Tax Efficiency: With tax-deferred growth and the ability to take tax-free loans and withdrawals, IUL provides a tax-efficient way to grow and access your wealth, making it a superior choice compared to traditional retirement accounts.

Real-Life Success Stories

Consider the story of Mark, a 40-year-old physician. Mark earns $250,000 a year but felt the pressure of high taxes, student loans, and saving for his children's education. He decided to invest in an IUL policy. Over the years, the cash value of his IUL grew significantly, allowing him to take out a tax-free loan to pay off his student loans and cover a down payment on a house. The policy also provided peace of mind, knowing his family was financially secure if anything happened to him. Now, Mark's biggest worry is whether to get the beach house in Malibu or Miami. Tough life.

The Next Step for Future Wealth Builders

For Future Wealth Builders like Sarah, James, and Mark, understanding the benefits of IUL is the first step towards transforming their financial future. By leveraging the unique features of IUL, they can break free from the cycle of high spending and low saving, ensuring a secure and prosperous future for themselves and their families.

Conclusion

Future Wealth Builders are in a unique position with their high income but limited savings. Indexed Universal Life Insurance (IUL) provides an ideal solution to address their financial challenges and opportunities. By incorporating IUL into their financial plan, Future Wealth Builders can achieve financial security, build wealth, and leave a lasting legacy for their families. It's time to stop spending and start saving with IUL, the perfect tool for those high earners still building their wealth.

And speaking of building wealth, let's flip the page and dive into how the truly high rollers — CEOs, athletes, entertainers — are leveraging IUL to secure their fortunes and build dynasties. Get ready for some jaw-dropping stories and killer strategies!

Chapter 13: The Rich & Famous: CEOs, Actors & Athletes

Introduction

High net worth individuals (HNWIs), like Fortune 500 CEOs, pro athletes, actors, and business moguls, face unique financial challenges. Managing substantial incomes, minimizing tax hits, preserving wealth, and planning for a cushy retirement are just a few. Indexed Universal Life Insurance (IUL) is a slick, flexible solution that can tackle these issues head-on. This chapter dives into how HNWIs can leverage IUL to hit their financial goals and secure their legacy.

The Unique Financial Needs of High Net Worth Individuals

HNWIs have complex financial profiles that need tailored solutions. They need to:

1.   **Manage Significant Income:** High incomes lead to hefty tax bills, requiring effective strategies to minimize Uncle Sam's cut.

2.   **Preserve Wealth:** Protecting and growing wealth over the long term is crucial to staying in the game.

3.   **Plan for Retirement:** Ensuring a comfortable retirement requires strategic planning and smart investing.

4.   **Transfer Wealth:** Efficiently passing wealth to future generations while dodging estate taxes is a big deal.

HNWIs often juggle multiple income streams – salaries, bonuses, dividends, capital gains – you name it. This complexity demands advanced financial planning to optimize tax efficiency and ensure their wealth grows. Plus, navigating the intricacies of estate planning to make sure assets are transferred smoothly and with minimal tax impact to their heirs is no walk in the park.

Moreover, HNWIs must maintain a lifestyle that matches their financial status. This calls for careful planning and investment strategies that protect their wealth and ensure future growth. IUL policies offer the flexibility and benefits needed to address these unique financial needs, making them a top choice for high net worth individuals.

Leveraging IUL for High Net Worth Individuals

Tax Efficiency

Managing tax liabilities is a top concern for HNWIs. IUL policies come with significant tax advantages:

- **Tax-Deferred Growth:** The cash value of an IUL policy grows tax-deferred, allowing investments to compound without immediate tax implications.

- **Tax-Free Loans:** Policyholders can access the cash value through tax-free loans, providing liquidity without triggering taxable events.

- **Tax-Free Death Benefit:** The death benefit is paid out to beneficiaries tax-free, ensuring that wealth is transferred efficiently.

Tax-deferred growth in IUL policies is a game-changer. By deferring taxes, policyholders can take advantage of compounding interest, significantly enhancing their wealth over time. This strategy allows investments to grow more rapidly compared to taxable accounts, where annual taxes can eat away at returns.

Additionally, the ability to access the cash value of an IUL policy through tax-free loans provides unparalleled financial flexibility. HNWIs can use these loans to finance large purchases, invest in new opportunities, or cover unexpected expenses without incurring tax liabilities. This feature ensures that policyholders can maintain liquidity and financial stability throughout their lives.

Wealth Preservation

For HNWIs, preserving wealth is just as important as growing it. IUL policies offer:

- **Market Protection:** The cash value growth is linked to a market index but includes a protective floor, shielding against market downturns.

- **Flexible Premiums:** Policyholders can adjust premiums based on their financial situation, providing flexibility in managing cash flow.

- **Lifetime Coverage:** Unlike term insurance, IUL provides coverage for life, ensuring long-term financial protection.

Market protection is a key advantage of IUL policies. While the cash value is linked to a market index, it is not directly invested in the market, providing a safeguard against downturns. This ensures that policyholders can benefit from market gains without the risk of significant losses during market declines.

The flexibility in premium payments also allows HNWIs to adjust their contributions based on their financial situation. During times of high income, they can contribute more to their policy, increasing the cash value and death benefit. Conversely, during leaner times, they can reduce or even pause premium payments without losing coverage. This adaptability makes IUL an attractive option for those with fluctuating incomes.

Example: Professional Athletes

Professional athletes often face a short window for career earnings and high tax rates. By investing in an IUL policy, athletes can grow their wealth tax-deferred and access funds tax-free during their retirement. This strategy provides financial stability and protects against the volatility of their professional careers.

Consider a professional football player whose career lasts just over three years on average. During this brief period, the athlete may earn millions but also face substantial taxes. By investing a portion of their earnings in an IUL policy, the athlete can ensure that their wealth continues to grow tax-deferred even after their playing days are over.

The tax-free loan feature of IUL policies provides financial flexibility during retirement. The athlete can access their accumulated cash value to maintain their lifestyle, invest in new ventures, or cover unexpected expenses without incurring additional taxes. This strategy offers long-term financial security, allowing the athlete to enjoy their post-career years without financial stress.

At Breeze Wealth Management, several professional athletes on our client roster have benefited significantly from having IUL policies. By strategically investing in IUL, these athletes secure a more substantial retirement income than they actually accumulated while playing. One of our clients, a former NBA player, structured his IUL policy to ensure his post-retirement income surpasses his career earnings. This has provided him with a stable financial future, free from the uncertainties many retired athletes face.

Real-World Examples of Athletes

NBA Players:

      1.   **Allen Iverson:** Despite earning over $200 million during his career, Iverson faced financial troubles due to lavish spending and poor financial management. An IUL policy could have provided him with a structured way to save and grow his wealth, offering financial security post-retirement.

      2.   **Antoine Walker:** Walker earned over $108 million in his NBA career but filed for bankruptcy in 2010. Proper financial planning with an IUL policy could have helped him manage his wealth better and avoid financial ruin.

NFL Players:

      1.   **Vince Young:** Young made around $34 million in his NFL career but faced bankruptcy shortly after retiring. An IUL policy could have offered a safety net, ensuring his wealth continued to grow even after his playing days were over.

      2.   **Warren Sapp:** Despite earning $82 million, Sapp filed for bankruptcy in 2012. An IUL policy would have provided him with a more secure financial future, protecting his wealth from poor financial decisions.

MLB Players:

1.   **Darryl Strawberry:** Strawberry earned millions during his baseball career but faced significant financial difficulties due to legal and personal issues. An IUL policy could have safeguarded his earnings and ensured a stable financial future.

2.   **Curt Schilling:** Schilling earned over $114 million but faced financial ruin due to failed business ventures. An IUL policy could have preserved his wealth and provided a steady income stream during his retirement years.

Financial Illustration for Athletes

To illustrate the power of IUL, let's consider scenarios where athletes invested 10% of their average annual earnings into an IUL policy for seven years, allowing it to compound for 20 years thereafter with an average return of 8% based on the S&P 500. We'll also calculate how much the policy would pay them annually based on policy loans starting at age 50 until age 85.

Allen Iverson

- **Career Earnings:** $200 million
- **Career Length:** 14 years
- **Average Annual Earnings:** $14,285,714
- **Annual Investment (10%):** $1,428,571
- **Future Value After 20 Years:** $59,412,577
- **Annual Policy Loan (Age 50 to 85):** $3,628,428

Antoine Walker

- **Career Earnings:** $108 million
- **Career Length:** 13 years
- **Average Annual Earnings:** $8,307,692
- **Annual Investment (10%):** $830,769
- **Future Value After 20 Years:** $34,550,699
- **Annual Policy Loan (Age 50 to 85):** $2,110,070

Vince Young

- **Career Earnings:** $34 million
- **Career Length:** 6 years
- **Average Annual Earnings:** $5,666,667
- **Annual Investment (10%):** $566,667
- **Future Value After 20 Years:** $23,566,989
- **Annual Policy Loan (Age 50 to 85):** $1,439,276

Warren Sapp

- **Career Earnings:** $82 million
- **Career Length:** 13 years
- **Average Annual Earnings:** $6,307,692
- **Annual Investment (10%):** $630,769

- Future Value After 20 Years: $26,232,938
- Annual Policy Loan (Age 50 to 85): $1,602,090

Curt Schilling

- **Career Earnings:** $114 million
- **Career Length:** 20 years
- **Average Annual Earnings:** $5,700,000
- **Annual Investment (10%):** $570,000
- **Future Value After 20 Years:** $23,705,618
- **Annual Policy Loan (Age 50 to 85):** $1,447,743

Daryl Strawberry

- **Career Earnings:** $36 million
- **Career Length:** 12 years
- **Average Annual Earnings:** $3,000,000
- **Annual Investment (10%):** $300,000
- **Future Value After 20 Years:** $12,484,968
- **Annual Policy Loan (Age 50 to 85):** $761,178

These projections highlight how significant the growth can be with consistent contributions and the power of compounding interest. By investing a portion of their earnings into an IUL policy, these athletes could have ensured a robust financial safety net, providing long-term financial security and stability.

Conclusion

Imagine walking away from a stellar athletic career not just with memories, but with a guaranteed, tax-free income stream that lasts a lifetime. Indexed Universal Life (IUL) insurance makes this possible, offering benefits that traditional retirement accounts like 401(k)s and Roth IRAs simply cannot match. By leveraging the power of IUL, athletes can secure their financial future, ensuring that their wealth is protected and continues to grow.

Every athlete should consider working with an insurance advisor who has the expertise to set up these policies. This not only secures their own future but also the futures of their families. It's about making sure your financial security is **secured and locked down**. This approach ensures a prosperous future, free from the financial uncertainties that have plagued so many athletes post-retirement.

Next up, we'll explore how big banks have been using a similar concept to bolster their own financial security. Get ready to dive into the world of BOLI (Bank-Owned Life Insurance) in Chapter 14: BOLI: Corporate Strategies for Personal Finance. Discover how the financial giants are leveraging life insurance to secure their wealth and how you can apply these strategies to your own financial playbook.

Chapter 14: BOLI: Bank-Owned Life Insurance

Introduction

Alright, we've covered how high-net-worth individuals like athletes, actors, and CEOs benefit from Indexed Universal Life (IUL) insurance. But here's a plot twist — you don't need to be a millionaire or a superstar to reap these benefits. All you need to do is follow the breadcrumbs left by the biggest players in the game — banks.

Bank-Owned Life Insurance (BOLI) is a slick financial tool banks use to boost their earnings, provide employee benefits, and ensure long-term financial stability. This chapter explores the ins and outs of BOLI, its perks, and how you can use similar strategies with IUL for your own financial game plan. By understanding BOLI, you can leverage IUL to achieve tax-free growth, financial security, and strategic wealth management.

Definition and Basic Mechanics of BOLI

BOLI is when banks buy life insurance policies on key employees or executives, with the bank as both the owner and the beneficiary. The cash value in these policies grows over time, giving banks a reliable financial asset they can use for various purposes. Think of it as the bank's secret weapon for steady returns and a safety net.

Reasons Why Banks Invest in BOLI Policies

Banks aren't throwing money at BOLI for no reason. Here's why they're hooked:

- **Tax Advantages:** The cash value grows tax-deferred, and death benefits are received tax-free. Sweet deal, right?

- **Stable Return on Investment:** BOLI provides a steady, predictable return, perfect for riding out economic storms.

- **Employee Benefits and Retention:** The funds can be used to offer juicy benefits, helping to keep top talent happy and loyal.

Top Five Banks and Their BOLI Investments

To get a sense of BOLI's scale, let's peek at how the top five U.S. banks are investing in it:

1. **Bank of America**

   o **BOLI Holdings:** Approximately $24.1 billion

- Strategy: Supports employee benefits and manages long-term financial obligations.

2.   **Wells Fargo**

- **BOLI Holdings:** Approximately $18.4 billion

- **Strategy:** Generates tax-advantaged returns and funds employee benefit programs.

3.   **JPMorgan Chase & Co.**

- **BOLI Holdings:** Approximately $12.7 billion

- **Strategy:** Enhances financial stability and provides robust employee benefits.

4.   **Citigroup**

- **BOLI Holdings:** Approximately $9.8 billion

- **Strategy:** Maintains financial stability and offers attractive retirement plans for executives.

5.   **U.S. Bancorp**

- **BOLI Holdings:** Approximately $6.7 billion

- **Strategy:** Enhances earnings and offers competitive benefits to attract and retain talent.

Benefits of BOLI for Banks

Tax Advantages and Earnings Benefits

The tax perks of BOLI are huge. The cash value grows tax-deferred, so banks can compound their earnings more efficiently. Plus, death benefits come tax-free, giving banks a financial boost when they need it most. This tax efficiency makes BOLI an attractive investment.

Enhanced Liquidity and Capital Management

BOLI gives banks enhanced liquidity because they can tap into the cash value for various needs. This flexibility helps banks manage their capital better, especially during economic downturns or when new opportunities arise.

Employee Benefits and Executive Compensation

BOLI funds can be used to offer competitive benefits like supplemental executive retirement plans (SERPs) and deferred compensation plans. This helps banks attract and retain top talent, aligning their incentives with the bank's long-term goals.

Learning from BOLI: Applying Corporate Strategies to Personal Finance

Parallels Between BOLI Strategies and Personal IUL Policies

Just like banks use BOLI for tax-advantaged growth and stability, you can use IUL for similar benefits. IUL policies offer life insurance protection and cash value growth based on a market index. By understanding BOLI principles, you can apply these strategies to your personal finances, achieving greater security and growth potential.

Using Life Insurance for Tax-Free Growth and Income

IUL policies let your wealth grow tax-deferred. The cash value increases based on market performance but with protections against losses. You can access this cash value tax-free through loans, giving you a flexible and efficient way to manage your money.

Case Study: Successful BOLI Implementations

Real-World Examples of Banks Leveraging BOLI Effectively

Take a regional bank that significantly improved its financial stability and employee benefits through BOLI. By investing in BOLI policies, the bank generated tax-advantaged returns, enhanced liquidity, and offered better retirement plans for executives without affecting its cash flow.

Lessons Learned from Corporate Strategies

Individuals can learn a lot from these corporate strategies. By adopting similar approaches with IUL policies, you can achieve tax-free growth, financial stability, and protection against market volatility. Understanding and applying these principles can help you build a more robust financial plan.

Implementing BOLI Principles in Personal Finance

1. **Assess Your Financial Goals:** Know what you're aiming for. Whether it's retirement, education, or legacy planning, clear goals guide your strategy.

2. **Choose the Right IUL Policy:** Work with a savvy advisor to find the best policy for you. Look for the right mix of benefits, costs, and flexibility.

3. **Understand the Cash Value Accumulation:** Your cash value grows based on a market index, with caps on interest and floors for protection. Know the mechanics to manage your expectations and maximize benefits.

4. **Use Policy Loans Strategically:** Take advantage of tax-free loans against your cash value for big expenses, investments, or emergencies. This keeps your growth potential intact.

5. **Regularly Review and Adjust Your Strategy:** Financial planning isn't a one-and-done deal. Regularly check your policy's performance and adjust your strategy as needed.

Conclusion

Understanding and applying BOLI strategies can supercharge your personal financial planning. Leveraging life insurance for tax-free growth and stability isn't just for banks — it's a powerful tool for individuals too. Just as banks use BOLI to their advantage, you can use IUL to build a secure and prosperous financial future. With careful planning, strategic use of cash value, and regular reviews, IUL can be the cornerstone of a rock-solid financial plan.

But we're not stopping here. Next up, we're diving into the nitty-gritty of why you really only fail when you fail to plan. Ready to avoid common pitfalls and master your financial destiny? Buckle up for Chapter 13: You Only Fail When You Fail to Plan. Let's make sure your financial strategy is bulletproof.

Chapter 15: Stop Waiting For The Stars To Align: Take Action

Alright, folks, buckle up! We're diving into the ultimate playbook for taking control of your financial destiny with Indexed Universal Life Insurance (IUL). This isn't your grandma's savings account — this is a powerhouse strategy that, when done right, can transform your financial landscape. Whether you're young, middle-aged, or in the twilight years, we've got the moves to make your money work harder for you. Ready to flip the script on your finances? Let's get into it!

Understanding the Window of Compounding Interest

Explanation of Compounding Interest and Its Benefits

Here's the scoop: compounding interest is like financial steroids. Your money makes money, and then that money makes even more money. The earlier you start, the more your investments can balloon over time. It's like planting a tree today and reaping a forest in the future.

Impact of Starting Young vs. Starting Older

Younger folks, you've got the golden ticket. Starting early means your money has decades to grow. It's the financial equivalent of a head start in a marathon. But if you're a bit older, don't sweat it. You might have to sprint a bit faster, but with smart strategies, you can still cross the finish line in style.

Age and Contribution Strategies

Young Investors (20s and 30s)

Advantages of Starting Early

Listen up, young guns! Starting early means lower premiums, more flexibility, and a whole lot of growth potential. Think of it as getting into Bitcoin before it blew up.

Suggested Contribution Amounts and Growth Potential

Even if you're just tossing in $200 a month, over 40 years, that can grow into a small fortune. It's like trading a few coffees a week for a luxury retirement.

Mid-Life Investors (40s and 50s)

Adjusting Contributions Based on a Shorter Time Frame

Okay, mid-lifers, time to crank it up a notch. You might need to pump in more cash now, but the growth is still very much within reach. Think of it as turbocharging your financial engine.

Strategies to Maximize Growth Despite a Later Start

Don't just dump all your eggs in one basket. Mix IUL with a well-rounded portfolio of stocks and bonds. Diversification is your secret weapon. Plus, it's like having a financial safety net for those unexpected life curveballs.

Late-Life Investors (60s and Beyond)

Higher Contributions to Catch Up

Late to the game? No worries. You'll need to play catch-up, but with higher contributions and a focus on steady growth, you can still secure your financial future. Think of it as a final sprint to the finish line.

Ensuring Financial Protection and Legacy Planning

IUL isn't just about growing wealth; it's about protecting it too. Use the policy's death benefit to ensure your loved ones are taken care of. Plus, you can tap into the cash value for unexpected expenses—like that sudden urge to buy a yacht.

Health and Qualification

Importance of Health in Qualifying for IUL Policies

Your health matters, big time. Better health means better rates and higher benefits. It's like getting VIP access to the financial club.

Tips for Improving Health to Qualify for Better Rates

Eat right, exercise, quit smoking, and get regular check-ups. Treat your body like the temple it is, and your wallet will thank you.

Steps to Get Started with IUL

Assessing Financial Goals and Needs

Start with a clear picture of what you want. Retirement in Bali? College funds for the kiddos? Knowing your goals helps tailor your IUL policy to fit like a glove.

Finding a Knowledgeable Advisor

Don't go at it alone. Find a financial advisor who knows IULs inside and out. Make sure they're not just a slick talker but have your best interests at heart.

Comparing IUL Policies and Providers

Shop around. Compare policies, benefits, and costs. Look for the best deal like you're hunting for Black Friday bargains.

Setting Up and Maintaining the Policy

Once you've found the right policy, get it set up and stay on top of it. Regular premiums, regular reviews — keep it humming like a well-oiled machine.

Maximizing the Benefits of IUL

Regular Reviews and Adjustments

Don't set it and forget it. Regularly review your policy with your advisor. Make tweaks and adjustments as your life and financial situation evolve.

Using Policy Loans Strategically

Need cash? Don't raid your savings. Use policy loans strategically. It's like having a financial Swiss Army knife — versatile and handy.

Balancing IUL with Other Financial Strategies

Don't put all your eggs in one basket. Balance your IUL with other strategies as well. A balanced approach is your ticket to financial zen.

Conclusion

Alright, it's go time! Stop procrastinating and start taking actionable steps with IUL today. This isn't just another chapter — it's your call to action. The sooner you jump in, the sooner you can start building a fortress of financial security. So, pick up the phone, call a knowledgeable advisor, and get the ball rolling. Your future self will thank you.

Securing Your Financial Future with IUL

Alright, let's cut to the chase. If you've made it this far, you're serious about taking control of your financial future. Indexed Universal Life (IUL) insurance isn't just another fancy financial product; it's a powerhouse that can change your life. It's like having a Swiss Army knife for your finances — versatile, reliable, and packed with features that can help you build wealth, plan for retirement, and protect your family's financial future.

Think of IUL as your financial bodyguard. It's there to protect your assets, grow your wealth, and ensure that when life throws a curveball, you're not left scrambling. By tying the growth potential to market performance while safeguarding your cash value from market downturns, IUL stands out as a financial superhero.

Whether you're a young professional looking to build a solid foundation, a seasoned investor seeking a smart addition to your portfolio, or someone planning to leave a legacy, IUL has something for you. It's flexible, powerful, and adaptable — just like you need to be in today's unpredictable world.

Here's the kicker: Successful financial planning isn't about getting lucky; it's about making smart, informed decisions. IUL isn't a magic bullet, but with the right guidance and a solid understanding of your financial goals, it can be a game-changer. It's about playing the long game and staying ahead of the curve.

So, thank you for sticking with me through this journey. I hope this book has not only demystified the complexities of IUL but also inspired you to take bold steps toward securing your financial future. Now, go out there and secure & lock down your financial destiny like the rockstar you are. Cheers to your financial freedom and prosperity!

References

1. **Andrew, D. (2020).** *The Laser Fund: How to Diversify and Create a Foundation for a Tax-Free Retirement.* Emperial Publishing.

2. **Bogle, J. C. (2007).** *The Little Book of Common Sense Investing: The Only Way to Guarantee Your Fair Share of Stock Market Returns.* Wiley.

3. **Buffett, W.** Quotes and investment principles from Warren Buffett, sourced from various interviews and his annual letters to shareholders.

4. **Feldman, S. D. (2015).** *Retirement Planning with Indexed Universal Life Insurance: How to Secure a Tax-Free Income for Life.* Independent Publisher.

5. **Hunt, B. (2018).** *The Secret Power of IUL: How to Grow Your Wealth and Secure Your Future with Indexed Universal Life Insurance.* Financial Freedom Press.

6. **Kelly, P. (2011).** *Tax-Free Retirement.* Independent Publisher.

7. **Luu, S.** Insights and strategies from Shirley Luu, sourced from her talks, seminars, and book *I.U.L ASAP!*

8.   **Malkiel, B. G. (2003).** *A Random Walk Down Wall Street: The Time-Tested Strategy for Successful Investing.* W. W. Norton & Company.

9.   **McKnight, D. (2018).** *The Power of Zero: How to Get to the 0% Tax Bracket and Transform Your Retirement.* Crown Business.

10.   **Robbins, T. (2014).** *Money: Master the Game - 7 Simple Steps to Financial Freedom.* Simon & Schuster.

11.   **Sapaula, M. (2021).** *The 7-Figure IUL: How to Create a 7-Figure Tax-Free Retirement Income Using Indexed Universal Life Insurance.* Wealth Solutions Press.

12.   **Hegna, T. (2011).** *Paychecks and Playchecks: Retirement Solutions for Life.* Acanthus Publishing.

About the Author

Brandon Beal

Brandon Beal is not just a financial strategist; he is a visionary leader and the driving force behind Breeze Wealth Management. With an unwavering commitment to empowering individuals and families, Brandon has dedicated his life to transforming the landscape of financial planning and wealth management.

Armed with unparalleled expertise in Indexed Universal Life insurance (IUL), Brandon has emerged as a beacon of knowledge and inspiration in the financial industry. His dynamic approach and profound insights have made him a sought-after advisor and speaker, revered for his ability to simplify complex financial concepts and craft innovative strategies that pave the way to financial freedom.

Brandon's mission is nothing short of heroic: to guide his clients through the financial labyrinth and ensure they achieve lasting security and prosperity. His relentless pursuit of excellence and his dedication to demystifying the intricacies of wealth building have earned him the trust and admiration of countless individuals.

Beyond his professional accomplishments, Brandon is a devoted family man who cherishes every moment with his loved ones. When he's not forging financial futures or captivating audiences with his expertise, you'll find him staying active, exploring new horizons, and continually expanding his knowledge in the ever-evolving world of finance.

Brandon Beal is more than an advisor; he is a champion of financial empowerment, a master strategist, and a relentless advocate for those striving to secure their financial destiny. Join him on this journey and unlock the potential to achieve your own financial triumphs.